HOME
ALIVE

HOME ALIVE

MUST Strategies for Surviving Encounters with the Police

Copyright © 2019 by Geoffrey Mount Varner and Brooke Varner. All rights reserved

Published by Amazon Create Space

All rights reserved. No part of this publication may be reproduced, distributed, or transmitted in any form or by any means, including photocopying, recording, or other electronic or mechanical methods, without the prior written permission of the publisher, except in the case of brief quotations embodied in critical reviews and certain other noncommercial uses permitted by copyright law. For permission requests, write to the publisher, addressed "Attention: Permissions Coordinator," at the address below.

Limit of Liability/Disclaimer of Warranty: While the publisher and author have used their best efforts in preparing this book, they make no representations of warranties with the respect to the accuracy or completeness of the contents of this book and specifically disclaim any implied warranties or merchantability or fitness for a particular purpose. No warranty may be created or extended by sales representatives or written sales materials. The advice and strategies contained herein may not be suitable for your situation. You should consult with a professional where appropriate. Neither the publisher not author shall be liable for damages arising here from.

Lifeline Medical Consulting, LLC

Bowie, Maryland

www.drsavinglives.com

For more information about special discounts available for bulk purchases, sales promotions, educational needs and speaking engagements email info@drsavinglives.com or visit us at drsavinglives.com.

ISBN - 978-0-9980336-3-1

ISBN - 978-0-9980336-4-8 (Ebk)

Format: Paperback

Page Count: 128

Product Dimensions: 5.5 x 0.3 x 8.5 inches

Publication Date: January 4, 2019

Second Edition

Printed in the United States

FORWARD

Dr. Geoffrey Mount Varner has written the best book that I wish never had to be written. This book of advice and warning speaks in very clear term to the continued unfortunate reality that too many young boys and men of color are prejudiced against in their interactions with those sworn to protect and serve. As a physician, father, community activist, teacher, and person of faith, Dr. Mount Varner's intent is compelling and clear that ever person, police and civilian, deserves the right to come home safe.

Dr. Mount Varner presents a holistic view of the physical, physiological, community, and spiritual impact on the unnecessary loss of life. The practical advice he gives to young boys and men can help them live to become the grandfathers and great grandfathers they can become by simply coming home safe each night. It is unfortunate that boys and men of color have to be more cautious than others and we must work on all fronts including political to change this ethos. Until the political and cultural context is changed the lessons of extraordinary caution have to be given.

This book is compelling and compassionate and should be a part of the discourse between parents and children, religious leaders and congregants, and community leaders and citizens. It should be a part of the reading of police officers and first responders. Dr. Mount Varner wants everyone to be able to end their day safe and at peace with themselves and others.

U.S. Ambassador to the African Union, Michael A. Battle, former President of Interdenominational Theological Center (ITC)

TABLE OF CONTENTS

Introduction		ix
Chapter 1	God Bless America	1
Chapter 2	The ER: Each Life Helps to Save Another Life	11
Chapter 3	Everyone Home Alive Safe and Unharmed	18
Chapter 4	The 11 Rules That Will Save Your Life	22
Chapter 5	Black Males Part 1 - Treated Differently	86
Chapter 6	Black Males Part 2 - It's Going to be Okay	95
Conclusion		102
References		111

INTRODUCTION

"Ouch, stop hitting me!" I could hear the man scream and the loud whack that came with each hit. I heard a voice say, "I told you not to move." Another whack and then another scream of agony. I went into the exam room in the Emergency Department where I was working as an emergency medicine physician. There was blood everywhere. And there were two angry men, an officer and a young man handcuffed to the gurney. The gentleman handcuffed to the gurney was the patient. Let's name him Paul.

Paul had an acute large deep cut over his right eyebrow. The dressing that had been placed there to control the bleeding had come off. As I walked in, I introduced myself and let them know that I was the ER doctor who would be taking care of Paul. I also applied several new dressings to Paul's forehead to control the bleeding. Paul jumped up and started yelling, "He keeps hitting me!"

The officer quickly grabbed him, put him back on the stretcher, and said, "I told you not to move."

Paul was 19 years old and was under arrest. He was clearly distressed and agitated. The officer was agitated, vigilant, and seemed quite angry too.

I asked what had happened. By both accounts, Paul was being chased on foot by the police, and when he turned the corner, there was a piece of metal sticking out. The metal caused the big gash on his forehead, which immediately bled profusely. Paul said, "I could not see because of the blood, and then they scooped me."

While I was attempting to examine him, Paul kept interrupting and moving his head in defiance. I slowed the room down and compassionately, with the officer present, I explained to Paul, "I have nothing to do with the police. My only purpose is to help and treat you." Paul immediately directed a tirade of curses toward me and again tried to get up and off of the stretcher. It was okay because I knew Paul was upset at the situation and not really at me. But the officer again quickly grabbed him and threw him on the stretcher. I did not think Paul was trying to get off of the stretcher to hurt me or the officer, but I could see how the officer may have felt that he was. I went back and sat next to Paul, put my hand on his shoulder, and humbly and calmly pleaded with him to not move anymore. Just as I was about to have the officer wait outside of the room, as I normally do, the patient aggressively jumped at me. I let the officer stay. The officer had his baton out by now. I said to Paul, while simultaneously looking the officer in the eye, "I am sure that as long as you don't try to move, the officer will not hit you. He would have to explain to folks why he hit a calm, cooperative person in my presence." Paul immediately went into several expletives, but in the end agreed to stop moving.

While I was setting up my laceration tray, there was a great deal of mean-spirited back and forth between the officer and Paul. They talked about each other's mothers and what they would do to each other if they saw each other on the street and no one was around.

I had to leave the room to grab a few more supplies. I could hear them arguing as I walked away. A few minutes later, I heard a scuffle and then several whacks, followed by several shrieks of pain. I went back in the room, and the officer said, "I told him not to move."

Paul said, "I told him I was going to f*** him up."

I cleaned and irrigated Paul's laceration and began to suture it. Paul and the officer were fussing the entire time. I needed to leave the room to grab more sutures, but I was scared the officer would hit Paul again.

INTRODUCTION xi

I thought about asking the officer to stick his head out and call for an ER tech, but I was scared what Paul would do. Just as I was about to break scrub, a nurse came in to say Paul's family was there to see him. I asked her to get me a few sutures.

The officer was concerned about who was there to visit Paul and called for additional officers on his radio. I finished all 24 sutures. Then I left the room to discuss Paul's care with his family. I found his mother, father, and sister at the nurse's station. They were appropriately concerned. The mother and sister were crying. I explained to the family that I had put in 24 stitches and that the wound lined up pretty well and I thought it would heal well.

Suddenly, we all heard three large whacks followed by angry, agonized groans of pain. Paul's mother immediately began to cry and yell, "What are they doing to my baby? They're killing him!" Her shrieks of fear vibrated through the entire ER. As I ran back to Paul's room, I found two officers carrying Paul out with his hands cuffed behind him. They had placed chains on his ankles, as well. Paul was violently struggling, kicking, and cursing as they carried him out.

Seeing her child that way, his mother loudly screeched and cried out in fear.

The officer told me, "We are going to put him in the wagon, and I will come in and get his discharge papers once we have him secured safely."

While Paul's ordeal was troubling, what really hit home for me were the looks of sheer terror on the faces of his family members as they sat there helpless to do anything about their loved one being hit by the officer. Their stares of horror seemed to occur in slow motion and replayed themselves over and over in my mind.

And this was not an isolated incident. I have witnessed many screams and hollers and pain. I've seen many families devastated by the impact of police killings and violent police interactions. That is what led me to begin the research for this book. I wrote this book for those families and others like them. I wrote this book so as few families as possible have to experience what those families have experienced.

Twenty years of emergency medicine are speaking now. What I'm about to say is not intended to be heartless or cold, but is simply a statement of fact: When we die, no matter the cause, we are gone. It is over. Yes, there will be funerals, dedications for some, and protest demonstrations for a few. But the dead are gone. The dead are not the ones who have to feel or bear the burden and the pain of being gone. The family has to endure the sustained pain. We have to carry that painful cross that will be with us forever.

We are the ones left with the why, what if, how could this happen, if only I had not let him go, I should have known better, I should have been there to protect him.

Let us do everything in our power to bring our children home alive. Yes, the primary objective of this book is to save lives. The book's approach is to foster understanding in our young loved ones that will allow them to greatly diminish the likelihood that they will be hurt or killed when they engage with the police. Most important, these are recommendations you can start using right now. There is no reason for any of you to endure the pain of an untimely death or the severe injury of a loved one.

Tears taste salty. They don't know race or religion. Tears don't care about the circumstances that caused the pain; they are still going to taste salty. Meaning, grief affects all of us humans. We are all going to experience the enormous an inconsolable pain that follows the injury or sudden death of a loved one. Pain hurts. It causes tears and tears taste salty for anyone

INTRODUCTION

who cries. This is a shared human experience. Home Alive's goal is to acutely stop the pain that results from a violent or deadly interaction with the police. This book is for people of any race, ethnicity, or religion who have a young person in their lives whom they love and whom they want to keep safe.

CHAPTER ONE

GOD BLESS AMERICA

"Those who don't know history are doomed to repeat it."
—Edmund Burke

I am a board certified emergency medicine physician. I am a graduate of Hampton University and Harvard School of Public Health. I write this book as a fellow American. I am on a mission to save lives on a larger scale than I am able to do by treating individual patients.
I am a father. I am a husband. I am an uncle. I am a brother. I am a nephew. I am a friend. I am a loved one. I am a son. I am a Christian. My mother holds a Ph.D. and is a retired Senior Executive Officer of the federal government. I am the husband of a federal contracts attorney. I am the younger brother of a woman who is a circuit court judge and the older brother of a woman who is a district court judge in the same county. I am the father of two and the uncle of seven. I am a mentor to many. My family and I are America. We represent what America creates when we create a better union that allows for the unfettered pursuit of happiness.
America the great. As beneficiaries of America's greatness, we have an obligation to participate in

maintaining and sustaining it. Greatness does not come without hard work. It is the result of everyone collectively doing his or her part. America is known for innovating, changing, improving. We are known for fixing problems that have threatened to disrupt our core principles, such as "life, liberty, and the pursuit of happiness."

We are known for being able to use temporary fixes while permanent solutions are being developed. For example, there's Dr. Charles Drew, an American surgeon, who during World War II developed a method of storing blood. With this stored blood, combat medics and doctors did not to have to rely solely on available blood donors during a big influx of wounded soldiers. They could give the stored blood to the soldiers immediately when they needed it. The blood served as a bridge until definitive care for the soldier was available. Without the stored blood, thousands of soldiers would have died.

Another example of American fix-it-now ingenuity is John Haven Emerson, whose iron lung invention in 1931 led to the development of a mechanical device known as the ventilator. A ventilator can breathe for a human when a human can't breathe. The ventilator serves as a bridge until the patient can breathe on their own, without which the patient would die.

We are Americans. We build bridges. If we can't fix it right now, we don't just sit and let the patient die. No, we temporarily give them blood or insert the ventilator, while we aggressively seek a solution that will heal the patient.

Home Alive, consistent with America's fix-it-now history, is a book that is meant to pack the wound that is bleeding right now: that of all the blacks and other youths who are being killed or harmed by the

CHAPTER ONE

police when there is no imminent threat, or where a non-fatal alternative is available.

In the last several years, the proliferation of mobile phones with video recorders has enabled us to document what we have always known—the mass killing of black men by the police. Additionally, we are now also able to see that it is not only black men who are being killed, but so are white and Hispanic men—though not at the same shocking rate.

Here are the numbers that led me to write this book:

In 2017, a total of 1,129 people were killed by the police – that is an average of 3.1 people per day, or one person every 8 hours.

- To provide a context:
    - Canada: 25 fatal shootings per year by the police
    - England and Wales: 55 people killed by the police in the last 24 years
    - Australia: "94 fatal police shootings between 1992 and 2011" (Lartey, 2015);
- "There were only 14 days in 2017 where no one was killed by the police" in the U.S. (Mapping Police Violence, 2018);
- 49 percent of the people killed by the police in 2015 were white, 26 percent were black, 17 percent were Hispanic, and 3 percent were "other" (Tate, 2016).
- In 2017, "Most of the unarmed people killed were people of color (48 were black, 34 were Hispanic, 2 were Native American, and 2 were Pacific Islander – 50 were white, and 11 were unknown)" (Mapping Police Violence, 2017);

- "Young black men were nine times more likely than other Americans to be killed by police officers in 2015" (Swaine et al, 2015);
- "Fewer than one in three black people killed by police in America this year were suspected of a violent crime and allegedly armed" (Mapping Police Violence, 2017);
- "The only thing that was significant in predicting whether someone shot and killed by police was unarmed was whether or not they were black ... crime variables did not matter in terms of predicting whether the person killed was unarmed" (Nix, 2016);
- In 2015, approximately 40 percent of police killings began as a traffic/street stop or a domestic disturbance (Swaine et al, 2015);
- The number of police officers convicted of a crime for killing a black person while on duty in 2014: zero (Mapping Police Violence, 2016)
- The number of officers convicted of murder or manslaughter charges in 2015: zero (Ferner and Wing, 2016);
- "In 2013, there were more than 100,000 injuries caused by law enforcement that resulted in hospitalizations or trips to the emergency department" (American Public Health Association, 2016);
- In July of 2018, Dr. Frank Edwards paper, Risk of Police-Involved Death by Race/Ethnicity and Place, Edwards reported, "....two-thirds of all the shootings we're finding are in suburban, smaller metropolitan and rural areas........."

CHAPTER ONE

You will observe that more whites were killed by police in 2015 than blacks or Hispanics. But whites make up 63 percent of the population, blacks make up 12 percent, and Hispanics and Latinos make up 17 percent. In other words, there is a disproportionate number of blacks and Latinos being killed by police as compared to whites. Additionally, a *Washington Post* investigation in August 2015 found that black men, who constitute six percent of the US population, account for 40 percent of the unarmed people fatally shot by police (Wong, 2016). In my final chapters, I will address the particular problems faced by black men. It is clear that black males are being killed at a highly disproportionate rate. However, as the stats above show, in sheer numbers, more white people than black people die in police encounters. Hence, I am writing this book for all youth, including white youth.

In December of 2015, Dr. Nancy Krieger, a professor at the Harvard School of Public Health, published a paper, "Police Killings and Police Death are Public Health Data and Can be Counted." In it, Dr. Krieger argues that one of the impacts of police violence is "... the toll taken on family members and the communities, both for persons killed by the police and for police killed in the line of duty." Krieger goes on to state, "A core premise of our proposal is that mortality and morbidity due to police violence is a matter of public health, not just criminal justice." Dr. Krieger is not alone in coming to this conclusion. There is a growing consensus in the public health community that police-related deaths constitute a public health crisis. The American Psychological Association, the American Academy of Family Physicians, the Student National Medical Association, and the American Public Health Association have all made similar findings. We can look at historical examples like malaria, smoking, influenza, HIV, domestic violence, and infant mortality to demonstrate that when a crisis has been addressed in the public health arena, there has always been significant measurable improvements within years. Government agencies, citizens, community organizations, and politicians have historically been known to align and rally behind public health crises and devote appropriate resources and attention to solving the problem. We must declare the problem of police killings a public health national emergency. Then the public health world will be able to help institute solutions.

But it will take years. Meanwhile, Americans are dying at the hands of the police on daily basis. Therefore, with this book, I am attempting to perform the same function I would as an ER doctor during any public health crisis: make the transfusion, get the patient breathing, staunch the flow of blood, stop the spread of infection, now, immediately, using the means most readily available to me.

The number of killings of blacks and young people of other races and ethnicities in this country is so high that until we solve the larger systemic problem underlying police killings, we need a survival manual for interacting with the police. This book is that manual, to be read, used, and taught—by not only the parents of black and Hispanic males, but by black and Hispanic males themselves. Frankly, all Americans, especially those who know a male, should read this book. It will save their life.

This book is not intended to solve the American crisis of deadly police citizen interactions. It also purposely does not address the underlying causes. It is meant to be a bridge while the larger permanent solutions are

CHAPTER ONE

being developed. As a community, we Americans must work hard and work together to undo those elements of our system that create the conditions in which police use unnecessary force, especially when interacting with black and brown civilians. That is the longer fix, and we are working on it. The short fix is: if you are a young person—especially a young black person—you must do everything you can to survive an encounter with the police. This book will equip you with the skills needed to stay alive.

Let me add that I am a police advocate. I feel strongly that the police are a part of the very fabric that helps to make this country great. We are a country of law and order. The police help maintain law and order, sometimes by force. We recognize that the job of a police officer, whether they are working for the city, state, or federal government, is one of the most difficult positions in the civil service. We thank them for their paid efforts. As the statistics about police injuries and fatalities show, police work is an inherently stressful and high-risk job. Officers are keenly aware that every time they make a routine traffic stop, or answer a commonplace domestic disturbance call, they are potentially putting their lives on the line.

Here is what the data shows:

- "There have been 64 law enforcement officers shot and killed nationwide in 2016 – the most in five years." (Gambrell, 2016).
- "There were 58,723 assaults against law enforcement officers in 2016, resulting in 16,677 injuries" (National Law Enforcement Officers Memorial Fund, 2018).

- "The leading circumstance of firearms-related fatalities were officers responding to domestic disturbances and conducting traffic stops" (National Law Enforcement Officers Memorial Fund, 2017);
- "Of the 1,146 people killed, about one in five were unarmed but another one in five fired shots of their own at officers before being killed." (Swaine et al., 2015);
- In 2016, 66 law enforcement officers were killed in the line of duty during a felonious incident:
  - 62 of the officers were killed with firearms 19 of the officers killed were zero to five feet from the offenders (National Law Enforcement Officers Memorial Fund, 2016).

All the more reason why this book's de-escalation strategies for civilians interacting with police are of paramount importance.

I am not in the camp that believes police are consciously bent on killing young black, Latino, and white folk. Quite the contrary. I have a long history of interacting with police officers, first as a young man and now as an emergency medicine physician. My experiences, as well as my faith, tell me that police are like most people, inherently good. However, presented with the wrong opportunity, at the wrong time, wrong place, and under the wrong kind of pressure, police, like most other people, will do the wrong thing.

Most officers start their day wanting to do good and do the right thing. However, their good intentions may be clouded by their unconscious projections. Travis Bradberry and Jean Greaves, authors of *Emotional*

CHAPTER ONE

Intelligence 2.0, sum it up well and crisply, "Everything you see—including yourself—must travel through your own lens. The problem is, your lens is tainted by your own experiences, your beliefs, and, without question, your moods" (Travis Bradberry, 2009). In other words, we let our past experiences impact our current involvement, often without being aware of this emotional hijacking.

As a community, including police officers, we have to learn to enter each situation with an objective mind to see beyond the biases superimposed by our past experiences.

I write this book based in part on my experience as an emergency medicine physician. My job is the acute management and stabilization of any patients who present to the emergency department. As such, I am not only a witness of history, but I'm a participant, as well. I am an observer of sins. I am viewer of the good, the bad, and the ugly of humanity. I am a person who fills the void when the toll of unfortunate circumstance or just plain bad luck manifests in your life or the life of a loved one. I am that person who searches through a patient's belongings looking for a next of kin to contact. I am the person who makes the phone call and lets you know the person you kissed in the morning and expected to see in the evening has had something very bad happen to them. For the past 20 years, my occupation has allowed me the privilege to witness our collective human experience from many different perspectives. I have had the opportunity to see the best and the worst of people. Through it all, my goal has been to save lives.

I decided to write this book with the same goal in mind: to save lives. For that reason, I have done hundreds of hours of interviews with law enforcement officers, attorneys, judges, and regular citizens, and I've done a great deal of reading and research. Based on a non-scientific meta-analysis of available information, combined with the insights of citizen activists, representatives of the state, and the people, I have determined that someone who uses the 11 lifesaving techniques I lay out in the following chapters will drastically decrease the likelihood of being killed or injured by the police.

Again, this book is not meant to be the cure for the societal problems that underlie the high incidence of police- involved deaths in this country. It is meant to save your life or the life of someone you love.

CHAPTER TWO

THE ER: EACH LIFE HELPS TO SAVE ANOTHER LIFE

> **"Be on your guard; stand firm in the faith; be courageous; be strong"**
>
> (1 Cor. 16:13)

As I explain each rule below, I will often use real-life stories from the emergency department to illustrate or serve as a paradigm of mutual understanding. Why? Because the ER is a microcosm of the human experience: life, death, injury, pain, suffering, joy, elation, relief, and humbling.

Visiting an emergency department is an experience that most Americans have had. That shared experience will help provide a context for many of the rules in this book. Often the circumstances that led us to the emergency department result in unforgettable feelings of pain, joy, suffering, relief, happiness, and even devastation.

It does not matter if you are young, old, male, female, heterosexual, bisexual, homosexual, rich, poor, smart, famous, black, Latino, white, Jewish, Muslim, Catholic or gentile. If your injury or illness is grave enough, all roads lead to the ER. The circumstances that lead to the ER humble the mightiest. At these moments, insights are often shared. Wisdom is learned and passed on.

And the ER is one of the few places in life where the playing field is equal and fair: it is not first come, first served, insurance or no insurance. Whoever is the sickest or most injured is seen first by the physician. This is a paradigm switch from the rest of life.

At times, once I explain to patients that I am not allowed to share with anyone else what they share with me, the emergency department world allows me to hear honest perspectives on the current circumstances. This confidentiality is protected; the court can't even make me divulge what I've heard unless it involves child abuse or the patient makes a specific threat to harm or kill a specific person. As we journey through this book, join me in learning from these real human experiences.

At 2:30 in the morning, the patient arrived handcuffed and with four officers holding him. Let's call him Phillip. Phillip had just been tased by an officer. Before central booking at the jail would accept him, the taser leads had to be removed and a physician of note had to state that he was medically clear.

Something was different about this man compared to the other police-tasered patients I had treated in the past. This gentleman was about 31 years old, well dressed, and polite toward me, but upset and very angry. It was a different type of anger than I was used to seeing. It was more of an indignation, humiliation, how-could-you-do-this-to-me type of anger.

Although the officers were in earshot of us, Phillip told me that he had stopped to grab a few bagels at the grocery store on his way to work. As he was leaving the store, he inadvertently bumped into a woman and caused her to drop her bag. He told me he apologized and tried to pick up her bag. A verbal, but very mean-spirited, argument ensued. Phillip gave her the middle finger and

CHAPTER TWO   13

then started to walk away, but the lady ran and caught him and maced him. He said that he was blinded and could not see anything and had to sit down. His eyes were red, and he became drenched with water someone had given him to try to clean his eyes out.

Moments later, the police arrived. When they approached Phillip, they had their hands on their weapons. They ordered him to put his hands up, turn around, and drop to his knees. Phillip said he was confused. He thought they were coming to see if he was okay. He said he turned around, but kept reaching for his eyes. He said, "My eyes were hurting and burning." He said he was fussing and upset. Phillip put his arms up again and then suddenly lowered them; at that point, he said he felt electric jolts going through his body. They had tased him.

Phillip's heart stopped, and he was no longer breathing. He was dying. The officers immediately initiated cardiopulmonary resuscitation (CPR). By the time the paramedics arrived, he had a pulse. As they prepared to intubate (place an endotracheal tube in the trachea), Phillip started to take spontaneous breaths. So instead of intubating, they placed a mask on his face, through which they administered 100 percent oxygen as they loaded him for transport to the emergency department.

On arrival, Phillip's vitals were stable, and he was alert and oriented. He was still visibly and verbally upset. He was placed on a cardiac monitor, and a cardiac evaluation was initiated. I removed the taser leads from his back and gave him a tetanus shot.

Additionally, I informed Phillip of all the events—the near-death and CPR. Phillip said, "I do not understand why the police tried to kill me."

During my debriefing with the police concerning the timeline of events—including the tasing, the CPR, their transport, and arrival—the officers confided, "We were scared to death that he was going to die."

Since we were sharing, I decided to ask, "Why did you all tase him?"

The officers opened up, saying, "We got a call about a black male who had attacked a woman." They went on to say, "Had he just listened to us, we would have been able to sort everything out. We really did not know what was going on. All we saw was an angry man with red eyes and sweat all over him—we thought he was on drugs and he just would not listen ... We later found out the facts, but, at that moment, we thought we were dealing with a drug-crazed patient on PCP or something."

When I spoke further with Phillip, he admitted, "I was just thrown off that the officers were treating me like I had done something wrong. I was the one who was maced; they should have been arresting the white woman who maced me."

Phillip was admitted to the hospital. On discharge the next day, officers took Phillip to the police station for additional information and did not press charges. The lady who maced him was charged with a misdemeanor.

The point of the story: We don't know when and where the police are going to arrive in our lives. We don't know what form or under what circumstances our interactions with the police will occur. We have to be prepared so we will not be surprised. In creating our readiness, we have to have immediate access to a set of rules that will help guide us through the interaction

CHAPTER TWO 15

with the police. *It does not matter if you are right or wrong.* There are specific ways that you must engage with the police during the initial encounter. We all think it is not going to happen to us. The truth is, you will have an interaction with the police; you just don't know when.

Life will happen to each and every one of us at the most surprising moments and least opportune times. It will strike us with unforeseeable and unpreventable events, including morbidity and mortality. There are also predictable events that we *can* prevent. We all have an unwritten social contract to help one another. This includes assisting in the prevention of injury and death of our brothers and sisters. Communal social contracts and awareness are not new. We only have to look at campaigns like "Don't do drugs," "Each one teach one," Amber alerts, and campaigns surrounding domestic violence. Also, when I speak of brothers and sisters, I mean the entire human race, regardless of color, race, religion, or ethnicity.

Our communities are facing an ever-growing threat: the rapid increase in documented and undocumented negative interactions, sometimes resulting in death, between the police and our youth. My goal in writing this book is not to cast aspersions or blame. In fact, it is quite the opposite. Regardless of your own personal leaning or ideology regarding the rise of citizen deaths at the hands of the police, it is my intention to provide you with the most effective life-saving strategies to maximize the likelihood that you and your loved ones will make it *home alive* and unharmed after interacting with the police. I have a son, several nephews, and many other young loved ones. It is my goal to arm our youth with critical rules that, when applied, will save their lives before, during, and after their interface with the police.

A few of the rules that follow are going to make you quiver or might even upset you. That's okay. Please read them anyway, and as you do, please stay mindful of the goal, *to make it home alive and unharmed.* Often, our youth are overwhelmed with the need to be validated or respected. And I agree with them that they should be respected. But, unfortunately, life is not fair, and wanting to be validated and feel respected is likely to hinder a person's ultimate goal of making it home safely and unharmed from an encounter with the police. At any given time, Mr. Respect may be absent, and you may just have to step up and say, "This is not my day to be respected by the police." Yes, I know this may sound harsh, but our kids and loved ones are being killed. And no matter who pulled the trigger, there are often actions the killed person could have taken to de-escalate the situation before the first shot was fired. Before you say it, in no way am I suggesting that any of the deaths were the dead person's fault.

In the interest of saving lives and decreasing morbidity and mortality, I am tactically *not* addressing the inequality that exists in the way police treat different groups of people. The disparity in treatment is decisively *not* the subject of this book. The point of this book is that during this period of history in which there are so many documented police killings, we, as citizens, have to go above and beyond what should be necessary in order to be sure that our loved ones make it *home alive.* Hence, these rules are not intended to leave our egos and self-esteem intact. They are intended to bring our children home with their bodies intact.

CHAPTER TWO

I know this seems strange and counterintuitive, but I have personally treated, counselled, and mourned with the parents of hundreds of youth who, had they just walked away from a conflict, would be alive today.

For my kids and nieces and nephews, if they make it home unharmed, I can accept that the police made them feel demeaned or treated them as sub-humans. I can fix their egos when they get home, and then we can fix the whole situation together. But I can't fix or heal anything if they're dead.

It is my experiences as an American, an ER doctor, a father, an uncle, a mentor, and a protégé that led me to write this book. I hope it will be one small contribution to saving lives.

CHAPTER THREE

EVERYONE *HOME ALIVE*, SAFE, AND UNHARMED

The police are part of the very foundation that helps to make America great. We are a country of law and order. The police are the necessary force behind the order. They are paid to do very difficult jobs. They are paid to run into life-threatening situations, while others are running away. They are the ones who in the fell clutch of circumstance serve as a bridge to safety. Their presence allows us to sleep comfortably at night, and they help create a country that is safe for our kids and loved ones to live in. Being a son, husband, father, brother, and friend, I can unabashedly proclaim that I am a police advocate. I need the police around. My loved ones are safer because of the police. I love the police because when I am travelling and my daughter calls to tell me she heard a noise in the basement, I know she can call them.

Have you ever thought about why your child or loved one can go to the movies, school, or walk down the street? Yes, on a cognitive and emotional level, you know that if anything goes wrong, our protect-and-serve heroes will be there to defend your loved ones. Wayne Kyle from *American Sniper* puts it best. There are three types of people in the world: sheep, wolves, and sheepdogs. The sheep are the meek and innocent. The wolves are the aggressive killers.

CHAPTER THREE

The sheepdogs protect the sheep from the wolves when the wolves are about to strike. It is the sheepdogs' job to protect good from evil (*American Sniper*). Ideally, the police are the sheepdogs. They are our heroes.

At the same time they are playing the crucial role of sheepdogs, police are also human beings. Police personnel have mothers, fathers, wives, husbands, friends, and kids who are depending on them to make it home each evening alive and safely, just as civilians do. The difference is that police have to make split-second decisions that could mean life or death for themselves and those around them. The purpose of the rules that follow is to create a synergy that will give all sides the greatest likelihood of seeing their loved ones again.

The police make me safer in my work as an ER physician, too. A few years ago, while I was working the night shift in the emergency department, a group of people dropped off a gunshot victim at the back door. Let's call the patient Thomas. Thomas had been shot in the abdomen. We went out and got Thomas from the ambulance bay and initiated our Advance Trauma Life Support (ATLS) protocols, which included cutting off his clothes. The patient was severely intoxicated on PCP and was very belligerent and aggressive. While he was being undressed, he grabbed a nurse and reached for his jacket. We immediately grabbed both the nurse and the jacket from Thomas. He was so strong it took six people to try to restrain him. The local police happened to be in the emergency department for a different matter and heard our yells and screams. They immediately assisted. The police and our hospital security team finally restrained Thomas, and from his jacket, they recovered a fully loaded Glock gun.

After restraining Thomas and while doing our clinical trauma workup on him, we were told that he had a family member who really wanted to see him. The patient was having X-rays taken, so I had time to go out and let the gentleman know that Thomas was in serious condition and we needed more time to finish our assessment before we could let family see him. The young man was very concerned and persistent, and he convinced me to briefly let him see Thomas. After all, if I had a loved one who was critically ill, I would want to see him right away too.

I escorted Thomas's cousin back, and as soon as the cousin saw the patient, his back arched, his pupils dilated, and he became visibly enraged. At that precise moment, an officer yelled, "Hey, what are you doing here?" and the man ran out of the emergency department with the police in pursuit. Later, an officer told me that the "cousin" was really a rival gang member, and when they caught him, he had a gun on him. The police said he had come to the hospital to finish killing Thomas. Had the police not been there, there could have been more gunshot victims, including myself and other ER staff. The police are there to protect and serve all of us.

I hope this story makes clear how much I value the police; they have very likely saved my life. At the same time, I am writing this book for one simple reason: citizens are being killed by the police at alarming rates, and the officers involved are almost always exonerated. It is not my purpose here to go into all the whys and wherefores of this grave problem. Suffice it to say that I am an advocate of police reform where needed.

But I also recognize that change does not happen overnight. While we are working in our communities to

CHAPTER THREE

help create that change, we must also respond to the here and now. We have to be honest with ourselves about the realities of our current situation. We must respond according to the way things are, not the way things should be.

So while we are working for the cultural adjustments and legal changes that will decrease tensions between the police and the citizenry, we must give our youth an additional armamentarium of skills for interacting with the police— tools that will help them make it *home alive.*

CHAPTER FOUR

THE 11 RULES THAT WILL SAVE YOUR LIFE

Survive Today So You Can Thrive Tomorrow!

After hundreds of hours of interviews with police, attorneys, judges, lawyers, and regular citizens, as well as extensive reading on the subject, I have developed the following 11 life-saving strategies. I will list them in this chapter and will elaborate on them in the remainder of this book. A common thread in the interviews, books, and articles is the need for communities to work together for the greater good. Get out of the silo view that only your child or family matters.

The childhood proverb, "All boats float in a rising tide," is true. It takes a village to raise a child. We have to be active partners in our communities. We should protect and care for one another. If you see your neighbor's son doing something wrong, you must speak to him and then visit his mother and/or father. We have to learn to be less scared of our own community partners, youth, and children. Christopher Wallace, also known as Biggie Smalls, noted the situation 20 years ago: "Back in the days, our parents used to take care of us. / Look at them now, they're even freakin scared of us. / Calling the city for help because they can't maintain / Damn things done changed" (Wallace, 1994). In short, we can't dread our offspring.

CHAPTER FOUR

We have to strengthen the control that we have over our youth. We can't fear them, and they must fear us. If our kids don't respect us, it is likely that they are not going to appropriately respect the police. But in the meantime, please read and discuss the strategies with your loved ones.

I recognize that many of you are going to disagree with at least a few of these rules. That's okay. Just having the discussion creates an opportunity for growth.

In short, this book is about split-second decisions. It prepares us to teach our kids how to make and prepare for decisions that have to be made during an acute situation. Most split-second decisions were made prior to the situation. Let's save our children.

Eleven MUST Steps Every Youth Should Follow When Stopped by the Police:

1. Do not run.
2. Admit to nothing.
3. Do not protest during a stop.
4. Be who you must be at that moment—be humble.
5. Obey the officer.
6. Make the officer feel safe—"pre-de-escalate."
7. No sudden movements and keep your hands out of your pockets.
8. Cry if you must.
9. Do not resist the officer.
10. When the driver is pulled over, everyone in the car is pulled over.
11. Be a superhero.

   Bonus Rule: Stay in your car.

Rule #1: Do not run.

> "Much evidence testifies that people who are emotionally adept—who know and manage their own feelings well, and who read and deal effectively with other people's feelings—are at an advantage in any domain of life."
> —Daniel Goleman, Emotional Intelligence (Goleman, 1994)

The patient was not in police custody when the paramedics brought him in. He was screaming in pain. The paramedics had already administered the maximum amount of morphine allowed under their protocols. But the loud shrieks of pain still resonated throughout the emergency department. Let's call the patient Luke.

Besides the fact that he was screaming in sheer pain, Luke appeared to be a healthy 20ish-year-old gentleman. His left ankle was turned completely around and dangling from his leg. Our first attempt at placing an IV to give Luke pain medicine failed.

The paramedics needed to leave to respond to another call. We attempted an IV a second time, and we failed again. This was made worse by the fact that we needed to move Luke off of the ambulance gurney to a hospital bed. Although we attempted to maintain in-line stabilization and support Luke's ankle while we moved him, Luke screamed in sheer terror and pain.

The pain was also making Luke sweat profusely. We took his blood pressure, it was 74/45—very low. We were concerned that he had lacerated a blood vessel in his knee and was bleeding inside his knee.

CHAPTER FOUR

Finally, we were able to place two large bore IVs and immediately gave Luke two liters of IV fluid wide open. His blood pressure improved and stayed stable. Orthopedics arrived, and, in the end, Luke was found to have fractured three bones in his ankle. The orthopedics resident said, "This is the worst ankle fracture I have ever seen ... the patient may not ever walk normally again."

The police later arrived and questioned Luke, but did not arrest him.

Luke said he had been walking home from work and two plain-clothes officers appeared out of nowhere and came running toward him, yelling for him not to move. Luke immediately ran, and a foot chase ensued. He fell into a ditch in the back of an alley. This was when he fractured his ankle. As a result of the fall and injury, the officers were able to catch him. Once they did, they realized he was not the person they were looking for. The officers called the paramedics for Luke and waited with him. When the officers asked, "Why did you run?" Luke candidly said, "You are the police; I just ran."

I saw Luke years later. As a result of his split-second decision to run, he had had six surgeries, walked with a cane, and appeared have put on a lot of weight since he was no longer able to run due to his injury.

The fight-or-flight response is the most basic survival function known to man, meaning that when confronted with threat, our brains are hard-wired to do one of two things: stay and fight, or run. This is also known as the acute stress response. It is our body's natural physiologic response to a perceived threat or harmful life event.

The fight-or-flight response causes the release of hormones—epinephrine, norepinephrine, and cortisol, among others. These chemicals are also known as sympathetic hormones and are released from the sympathetic nervous system. The sympathetic nervous system that all humans have is the same system that allows a deer to run from an oncoming predator and allows a lion to attack its prey. The chemicals released by this system cause an increase in heart rate, blood pressure, pupillary response, and a state of hyper-arousal. Cortisol can also cloud judgment.

There are numerous physiologic and socio-cognitive factors that may lead to fleeing from a police officer, but it is important to understand that once you do, the officer is likely to presume that you are guilty. That officer will now be chasing you, and his/her hormones will be rising in preparation for a physical confrontation that includes protecting himself from the fleeing "criminal" at all costs. It may be that past experience has given you legitimate reason to fear the police. Or you may be—or feel—guilty. The officer does not know any of this. The officer sees you running away and chases you, with his sympathetic nervous system kicking in.

Additionally, there is a strong likelihood that you will run from the police into an area that is away from the view of the general public. Then it becomes just you and the police. In case you happen to encounter one of those officers who are predisposed to doing you harm, it will be in the best interest of your health and life to stay in the public landscape.

Let me say again that a youth may have *a legitimate reason based on past experience to fear the police*, not necessarily because he is guilty, but because he or people he knows may have had negative experiences with police. For example, studies show that people of color have more contact with the police than whites, e.g., routine stops or requests for license, registration, and identification. For people of color, that means there are more touch points and, therefore, a greater likelihood of negative interactions with the police. Given that situation, if you are a person of color, it may seem all the more reasonable to run. But again, running will make the situation worse. Running will increase the likelihood of harm. We want our youth to emerge from any encounter with the police unharmed.

So what can we do about many of our youths' environmentally-conditioned response to run? We can alter it using techniques of behavioral modification. That will be a good way to minimize their impulse to run from the police.

Behavioral modifications are simple. In layman's terms, it goes something like this: If a known stressor generates a certain behavior, then we either change the stressor that leads to the response or we change the behavior that results from the response, or both. In this case, the stressor is the police. Changing police conduct at the systemic level is, as I have said, outside the scope of this book. So we will focus a little bit on changing individual police officers' responses to individual youths. But mainly we will focus on the youth's emotional response and behavior—the stress reaction and the running. It takes constant practice. By going through scenarios with our youths while at home, in church, in school, et cetera, we can change their learned reaction to run from the stressor, the police.

One approach to using behavior modification to alter a youth's flight response to the stressor—police—is to offer them repeated exposure to the police. If you're going to do this, it will be helpful to contact the community relations section of your local police department in advance to share with them your desire not to have your loved ones fearful of the police and see how willing they are to assist.

This repeated exposure should be a gradual process. You can start by driving the youth by the police station a few times on different days. You can then stop by the police station with the youth to ask about youth internships. Next, call the police department and ask if your child can come to the local police station with you and meet a few officers who patrol in the areas your loved ones frequent. The officers may also be willing to come to your church and meet or perhaps, if you request it, to your home. If the officers *are* willing to do this, you will then also be changing the stressor, that is, both the officers and your young person will be likely to have their fight-flight behavior modified through repeated friendly contact and familiarity.

Next, in your presence, have your child approach an officer and ask them basic questions, e.g., "What do I need to do to become an officer?"

Talk through and then run through different scenarios involving the police and *tell* the youth what he should do (this method of behavior modification does not require the presence of an officer, but if you have found one who is aligned with your interest in *making it home alive*, so much the better.). For instance, present this situation: "You and friends are walking down the street, chillin'. An officer approaches you and in a disrespectful manner says, 'Put your hands where I can see them.' At this point, you may be thinking, 'There is one of him and five of us, he can't catch all of us!' But he will probably catch at least one of you, so you will be increasing the chance that you or someone you care about will get hurt." Go over all reasons behind not running. Listen to their perspectives, too. Acknowledge that you've heard them. Answer them calmly. Present other scenarios, and walk them through their flight response and the reasons to resist it.

For every friendly interaction we are able to foster between our youths and the police, we are in essence changing the stimulus—the police—by making them less foreign or menacing through repeated positive exposures. We are also reducing the chance that a local officer will mistake our youth for a criminal. And by walking our youths through possible flight-inducing interactions with the police, we are changing the response to the stimulus, as well.

Home Alive tip #1:
Split second decisions are coming – prepare now.

Rule #2: Admit to nothing.

> "Practical intelligence... includes things like knowing what to say to whom, knowing when to say it, and knowing how to say it for maximum effect'...."
> —**Robert J. Sternberg, Practical Intelligence in Everyday Life**

It is important to be cordial and deferential. Answer the officers' questions the best you can without doing yourself harm.

But *be extremely cautious about admitting to anything.* It does not matter if it is a traffic violation, a civil infraction, a nonviolent criminal case, or a violent criminal case. There will come a time when guilt or innocence will be decided. The initial encounter with the police is *not* that time.

History is replete with examples of arrestees admitting to something that may not have been true. In the scary and traumatic moment of a looming arrest, people have been known to become discombobulated and say things and answer questions that unintentionally indict them, even when they are innocent.

Therefore, kindly and respectfully answer the officers' basic questions, but do not answer any questions about your guilt or innocence. For example, let's say you were at a party and you were part of a small fight that broke out, and then you left the party. Later, you are stopped by a police officer who asks, "Were you at the party?" You may choose to simply say yes. But it is not in your best interest to say, "Yes, and he hit me first, so then I hit him." The answer is a simple yes—there is no need to elaborate. Even after further urging

CHAPTER FOUR 31

by the officer, do not offer that you were involved in the altercation without having a lawyer present, or an adult who represents your interests. At some point, in an appropriate, non-confrontational, and deferential manner, you may need to ask, "Am I under arrest?" This signals to the officer that you are aware of your rights. If you are not under arrest, you are free to leave.

I must emphasize that an encounter with the police is not the time for chit-chat or small talk. You want the encounter to be as brief as possible and the communication to be as respectful and as official as possible.

A real life example from the emergency department underscores this rule. While I was working in the ED one night, the police brought in an 18-year-old male who was very combative—four officers had to carry him into the ED from the police car. Let's name him John. John was kicking and cursing at the police when they brought him into the exam room. He had an obvious bleeding frontal head laceration that needed to be assessed and sutured.

The officer told me that he had been in a "foot chase with the assailant, and when we caught him in the back of the alley, he resisted arrest. It took three officers to restrain the assailant, during which time he was punched in the face and head a couple of times. His clothes are wet because he tried to crawl under a shed, and we had to pull him out. I think he got the cut on his head when we pulled him from under the shed." Even after the patient was restrained and strapped to the stretcher, he continued to violently kick and was extremely verbally abusive to all six police officers in the room. The officers continued to ask John questions while he was still very agitated. I told the officers they needed to stop agitating the patient while he was under my care. Officers are usually very respectful when they bring patients to the hospital, and, as expected, when I asked them to stop antagonizing the patient, they did. It was not until John decided that he wanted to yell, converse, and antagonize the officers that they started to ask him questions again.

Again, I asked the officers to stay quiet while I did my history and physical. They complied, but John kept ranting and agitating the officers. I am comfortable with agitated patients. But John was different. He was a mean, angry, fuming type of agitated patient. Usually, I have the officers leave the room, but this time I did not because John appeared too frantic and unpredictable. As a result, and in fairness to John, I was mindful not to ask any questions that would possibly lead him to incriminate himself.

I ordered a few X-rays and CAT scans, which all came back negative. John was alert and oriented to person, place, and time during the history and physical. Thus, there was no need to order a toxicology screen because it was not going to change my management or disposition.

It took me 45 minutes to suture John's head laceration. In that span of time, the officers strategically antagonized John with a series of questions. He responded with a tirade. During the tirade, he said something that made one of the detectives suspicious. That detective called two more officers in, who further questioned John during one of his police-provoked outbursts, and he "just knew too many details about the crime for him to have not been involved." The police became convinced that John was the culprit.

Later, the police shared with me that they had originally had no suspicions about John being involved in the crime they would later charge him of committing. But they were able to maneuver him into admitting that he had information about the crime. As for John, when he and I were not in the presence of the police, he had confided in me that it was his brother who had committed the crime. He knew the incriminating details because his brother had shared them with him.

Conclusion: Had John stopped talking and not admitted to anything, he would not have been arrested or accused of a crime that he did not commit.

Again, this book is written in the spirit of the presumption of innocence. No one in this world is perfect, so I am pleased for whomever this book helps. But the last person you ever want to incriminate is yourself. Say as little as possible if you are innocent, especially if you are not as innocent as you would like to be.

Home Alive tip #2: Do not harm yourself—stop talking.

Rule #3: Do not protest during a stop—the officer has the power.

"**Power doesn't have to show off. Power is confident, self- assuring, self-starting and self-stopping, self-warming and self-justifying. When you have it, you know it.**"

—Ralph Ellison, Invisible Man

It is what Ellison does *not* say that is relevant to us here: know when you *don't* have power. During moments or periods when you don't have power, you are better served by being humble, deferential, and quiet. When you are in the courtroom in front of a judge, you have some power. When the police stop you, you don't. Ellison might have added that power is fleeting and mobile. You may not have power for the duration of your interaction with the officer, but be assured that you will regain power if you are able to leave the interaction not under arrest, unharmed, and alive.

The police have the government-sanctioned right to take your life. They have the right to be the judge, jury, and executioner all at the same time. Outside of God, no one has greater individual power in this country.

I'd like to address just young men here, since, as the statistics in my introduction show, young men are far more likely than young women to be harmed in encounters with the police. I understand that young men are ascending into adulthood, and that makes them want to assert their masculinity, and they may feel the need to let people know how manly or bold they are. But let's stop perpetuating the myth that our young boys are little men. I know many of them have had to mature early and assume manly roles in their households, but that does not make them men. It makes them mature boys.

Even from a neuronal perspective, boys' bodies are different from men's. Boys' brains and physiology are different. They are immature. This immaturity can be misleading. Let me give you an emergency department example.

I was working a midnight shift on a warm Friday night at a level one trauma center in an urban area. The emergency department fire and emergency medical services (EMS) radio alert sounded. The nurse answered the radio. EMS was calling to let us know that they had a "14-year-old male who had been shot in the chest but had stable vital signs ... Estimated time of arrival 15 minutes."

Our chest protects and contains our lungs, heart, and the largest vascular vessel that carries blood, the aorta. Whenever the heart and/or aorta are damaged from prolonged disease, infection, blunt or penetrating trauma, our blood pressure goes down. When our blood pressure goes down, our heart rate goes up, because our heart has to pump faster in order to keep enough blood circulating to maintain life.

A bullet to the chest means there is a high likelihood that the heart and/or aorta are injured, so the patient's blood pressure will be low and their heart rate high. These are signals to healthcare providers that the patient is critical and death may be imminent without acute intervention. Unstable vitals are akin to a general blowing the attack horn in a war: Everyone needs to stop what they are doing and come in and assist.

However, because the physiology of young people is different—more toned—their vital signs often will remain normal even when there is acute blood loss from a gunshot wound to the chest. That was the case with this 14-year-old boy. Despite having been shot in the chest, the young boy was sitting up on his stretcher in no apparent distress when EMS arrived at the hospital. His blood pressure was 120/60, and his heart rate was 72—i.e., they were normal.

    At 1:08 a.m., the boy arrived in the company of several police officers. We directed the EMS crew to the trauma bay. I had to ask all of the officers to step out of the room, and they kindly obliged. I introduced myself to the young boyish-looking patient—let's call him Simon—and took a brief history. He was quiet and gave short answers and was very hesitant. As usual, I had to explain to Simon that the physician and hospital staff had nothing to do with the police. "What you tell us does not go to the police," I told him. Surprisingly, unlike the other patients with chest wounds I have seen, he did not appear to be in pain. His vital signs continued to be stable. I did a quick history and physical exam and then let the police back in. I usually do not let the police in so soon, but I knew that he was likely going to die soon, and I wanted him to provide any information to the police that would enable them to find those responsible for the young patient's death. Simultaneously, the rest of the trauma team arrived, and I turned over care to the chief surgeon. I looked back at 14-year-old Simon before I left. He looked so innocent and clinically stable.

    I walked by the room about four minutes later, and I saw the boy boldly engaging the police in an argumentative posture. Simon had no idea that his combativeness with the police was irrelevant at that moment; he was in a fight for his very life and did not know it. I wanted to go hug him and say, "Son, you are probably about to die and don't even realize it. Is there anyone I can call? The only reason you are alive now for this long is because you are young and your body can maintain your blood pressure longer, even while you are bleeding into your chest cavity."

As I watched Simon, I witnessed an amazing act of compassion. The officer who the boy had just cursed gave his gun to his partner, took off his tie, and pulled up a chair next to Simon. Then he sat down, grabbed the boy's hand, and just held it. I could see him moving his lips, but it did not appear that any words were coming out. I could see the boy squeezing the officer's hand. A few minutes later, the surgical staff came to take Simon to the operating room (OR).

A total of about nine minutes went by from the moment Simon arrived to the time that the OR called for him. By the time the OR called, Simon's blood pressure had lowered and his heart rate had increased as a result of the blood loss in his chest. Had 14-year-old Simon been a 40-year-old, he would have probably been dead already. As he was being prepared to be rushed off to the OR, he developed a grey appearance and began to look scared. He waved at me as he went by.

It was reported later that on the way to the OR, patient Simon suddenly became unconscious, and the trauma team was not able to palpate a pulse. They began CPR, took him to the OR, cut his chest open, crossed-clamped the aorta, and delivered his heart from a pericardial effusion while simultaneously transfusing six units of blood and injecting epinephrine directly into his heart. It all happened quickly. Simon was pronounced dead at 1:23 a.m., 15 minutes after his arrival at the hospital. His family arrived shortly after.

Again, the shrieks of a screaming mother who was uncontrollably crying at the death of her child vibrated through the walls of emergency department and touched every soul who witnessed the worst day of her life. Yes, Simon was gone; he does not have to suffer. But his mother has to endure the burden of waking every day, subconsciously expecting her child to walk in. She has to wake up every morning and live the nightmare of the loss of a child. Until the end, Simon kept up a persona of "I am the man" during his police interview, and even during his interaction with the medical staff. I could see that he was behaving this way because he was scared and, therefore, was acting out. But I was left with many puzzling questions. Did he recognize that he had no power with the police who at that time were trying to talk to him? With the medical staff? What was it about his bravado that did not allow him to read the tea leaves? Why did he maintain the "I am the man" persona nearly all the way to his death?

Later, I pulled aside the officer who had held Simon's hand and bluntly asked, "What was that all about?" The officer let me know that he was "a former paramedic and I knew that the patient's gun shot was in all likelihood going to kill him. He was alone and appeared very scared. I have a son, too. Something told me to comfort him."

I told him how much I admired his actions. But I needed to know, so I asked, "What were you saying under your breath that made the boy squeeze your hand?" The officer said, "First I prayed, but then I let the boy know that I had a son his age and God told me to let you know that I love you the way a father loves a son, that I was going to sit by his side the way I would my own son." The officer and I shared a moment, dapped up, and from then on we chatted every time he brought a patient to the emergency department.

A boy dying so early from any cause is not right. It seems unnatural—like the sun not coming up one morning.

It was never reported in the news, and I was not privy to internal police documents, but what was described to me by an officer was that that young boy had been in a heated discussion with police officers earlier in the evening. Simon reportedly was verbally confrontational, and at one point, the officers were about to arrest him, but somehow decided not to. Later that evening, the same officers were the first responders to a domestic call. It happened to be the same boy, Simon, who had shown little deference to authority earlier in the evening. Simon reportedly appeared aggressive to the officers and "acted as if he was in charge of the situation." After he refused to comply with police instructions and multiple warnings, and after he suddenly reached for something, the police shot Simon. He was discovered not to have a weapon, although reportedly the officers thought he was reaching for a weapon.

You may argue that the world treats our boys like men, and, therefore, we should train them to be men. While I don't agree, I can follow your thought process. But as parents, we can't allow the world to define our boys. We can't change how the world treats our youth overnight, but we can change how our youth responds to the world. Let me be absolutely clear, once again: I am *not* blaming Simon for his own death at the age of 14, and I am not blaming his parents and mentors. I am trying to save lives here, so I am sharing this pain to illustrate my point that boys must be allowed and encouraged to be children and not to try to act like men.

Our boys are boys. We have to protect them. We must not train or allow our boys or girls to challenge the police during an encounter. It will be extremely counterproductive. In that situation, they have no power— zilch, nada, nothing, nil, zero. But as parents and mentors, we do have power. And with our power, we have to empower our kids not to argue, not to act out, not to show off, not to instigate, and not to agitate the police during a stop.

We have to remind them that they will regain their power *after the encounter with the police has ended.* To help drive home this point, we should teach them who their local state's attorney and/or district attorney is, who their chief of police is, who appoints the chief of police, who the chief of police answers to, who writes the training manuals, and who is the most senior officer assigned to address citizen complaints in our area. If your child has this fund of knowledge *before* an encounter, he will be less likely to act out *during* the encounter, because he will understand that avenues of redress will be available to him *after* the encounter.

Furthermore, tell your children that once they make it home, their greatest power is us—mothers, fathers, uncles, aunties, friends, mentors. We can now help them address anything that went wrong during the police interaction. There are a number of different routes available to us. Written complaint is the most often utilized. There are three common ways to complain: internal complaints, criminal complaints, and civil suits.

An internal complaint would mean writing a letter to the police department's captain and chief, the mayor, your local elected county official, your district attorney and/or state's attorney, your city administrator, the

ACLU, or all of the above. If you drop the letter off, be sure to get the name of the person you gave it to. Most times, there is an infrastructure in place, depending on the accusation, for the complainant (our youth) and the officer to meet face to face on neutral terms. At that time, you have just as much power as the officer. Those meetings can be very helpful and healing to both sides. And remember, officers hate having to do paperwork, and when complaints are filed against them, officers are forced to do a lot of writing, paperwork, and interviews. So even if your complaint is not upheld to your satisfaction, the paperwork alone may make the officer think twice about their behavior in the incident, and in subsequent incidents. And there will be a record in the officer's file. And if there is a trend of poor behavior, that will be documented in their file and hopefully addressed by their leadership.

For additional information on how to report police misconduct, visit *www.fbi.gov/investigate/civil-rights*.

The goal that we should teach our children to have when interacting with the police is not to "act like a man," but to do what you have to do make it *home alive*. If you are poor, it is even rougher. If you are black, it is hard, too. And if you are black and poor, the challenge is greater still—but far from insurmountable. Charles S. Dutton's character Mr. Butler in the movie *Menace to Society* said it best: "Being a black man in America isn't easy. The hunt is on, and you're the prey. All I'm saying is ... Survive! All right?" We must instill in them daily that the goal of each encounter, no matter the circumstance, is to survive!

Home Alive tip #3: *Doing your best may not be enough; do what is required to make it home alive.*

Rule #4: Be who you must be at that moment —be humble

> "Humility is not thinking less of yourself, it's thinking of yourself less."
>
> —Rick Warren, The Purpose-Driven Life

At the end of the day, officers want to feel respected. They have all the authority during an interaction. I keep highlighting *moments* because as soon as you make it home, the power dynamics change. Try this: Life is a movie that we are all living. A movie is made up of many frames or snapshots connected together to create the movie. When we extrapolate this example to the police, we should view our interaction during those moments with the officer as a series of snapshots, just one small piece of the movie. The beginning of the movie is the interaction, the middle is making it home safely, and the end is what you choose to do about the interaction if it was inappropriate or negative. When you leave the interaction with the officer—those few frames of the movie—alive, only then will you be able to finish writing the movie. You get to go and write, tell, and send your version of the movie to anyone and everyone. And if your movie does not line up with the officers' picture show, then at least you have a larger platform, audience, and support system (family, lawyers, and civil rights personnel) to exercise your power.

If there is any time to have on your Sunday best, it is during your encounter with the police. Sunday best means that you are as formal, kind, friendly, and accommodating as you can be. It does not matter if you are 9, 19, or 29. When dealing with the police, it is best and safest to be humble, respectful, deferential, and as courteous as possible.

CHAPTER FOUR

Yes, you do this even if the officer is inappropriate and disrespectful to you. You have to "yes sir/ma'am, no sir/ma'am," no matter what. In fact, there are four main answers when dealing with the police: yes, sir; no, sir; I don't know, sir; and no excuse, sir. Again, even if the officer demeans you and/or refers to you in a derogatory manner, you have to stay humble and respectful. You have to continue to answer in yes sir/ma'am or no sir/ma'am-type phrases.

I know this advice will not sit well with many of you, particularly people of color, because of how minorities have so often been portrayed in the past. For instance, let's look at a character like Stepin Fetchit.

Stepin Fetchit, a character played by the actor Lincoln Theodore Monroe Andrew Perry, was a controversial figure in popular culture in the early 1930s. His comic routine was centered on black folks being shiftless, lazy, dumb, and willing to do anything to please the white man, also known as boss man. No matter what the white man did or said to Stepin Fetchit, he would come back with a "Yyyeeeeesss, sir" or "Nnnooooo, sir." Stepin Fetchit was known for belittling himself to win the favor of whites. He would say or do almost anything to make boss man and those around him feel comfortable. His comic routine was so popular that Stepin Fetchit achieved superstar status during the 1930s. The flip side of that coin is that blacks resented the character because they believed that Stepin Fetchit fed into and built the stereotypes that blacks were weak and so dumb they would tolerate anything.

So let me be clear. I am in no way suggesting that youth be like Stepin Fetchit. I am proposing that they be as humble and as deferential, to the point that the officer is completely disarmed. Stepin Fetchit disarmed people. Gain strength in knowing that you don't have to be like Stepin Fetchit, but that doesn't mean you can't derive insight about using an extreme approach to get what you want. Stepin Fetchit's character was extreme, but Lincoln Perry, the actor who portrayed him, went on to become one of the first black millionaires of his day.

This bumbling buffoon-like character may have been what was needed for that period of time. But no longer. Dan Freeman, the title character in Sam Greenlee's novel, *The Spook Who Sat by the Door*, gives us a different perspective on approaches to dealing with dominant power structures.

In the novel, which was set in the late 1960s and early '70s, Freeman is a CIA agent, the token black within the agency. He is methodically, purposefully, and publically harassed by all levels of the power structure, also known as the federal government. Freeman is regularly humiliated in front of his peers and subordinates. But he strategically stays quiet. By enduring the humiliation, he is able to stay with the agency and be trained like all of the other agents. He then goes on to use that training and save thousands from similar treatment. Freeman trains a group of black men from Chicago, his hometown, in the techniques of guerilla warfare and propaganda he learned in the agency, and he then leads them in a revolution. The power structures treated and spoke to him in a disrespectful and humiliating manner. But he endured the individual moments of defeat in order to achieve a much greater victory in the long run. Your victory will begin in making it *home alive*

CHAPTER FOUR 45

and safely. In citing the example of *The Spook Who Sat by the Door*, I am not advocating a violent overthrow of the government. I am advocating stealth behavior in the interest of the long-term goal—to make it *home alive*.

My point: Staying quiet, controlled, and humble will likely keep you from being harmed, killed, or arrested, and thus will allow you to stay uncompromised. Yes, uncompromised! First and foremost, you were not killed. Second, you were not arrested, and, therefore, the testament you share about the incident later will be given more credence, as people will be far less likely to imagine you have any reason to lie. Additionally, in this era of social media, you get to testify about the officer(s)' behavior to millions.

No matter which tactic you choose, the goal is to get home safely. I would even say that your loved ones would pray that you be or act like whoever you need to in order to make it home safely.

Often in encounters with the police, if both parties take a "human pause," the outcome will be more favorable or compassionate. A human pause is a deep breath that helps to reset the situation. In some cases, it slows the speed of the situation and allows each side to see the other as a vital and equal part of the experience.

An example of this kind of pause is when citizens from other countries who speak English as a second language suddenly feign the inability to understand English in a stressful situation—especially when dealing with authorities. They now appear in distress and in need of help. Any momentum against them now slows down. It gives everyone a human pause and allows for hearts to soften and open.

So when youth are dealing with the police, it would behoove you to help create that human pause. First and foremost, it is essential to remain calm. The officer may be upset, may blame you, and assume that you are lying. Don't react. You have to appear so genuinely humble and deferential that the officer will be disarmed. The opening stanza of the poem "If—" by Rudyard Kipling sums it up best:

> "If you can keep your head when all about you
> Are losing theirs and blaming it on you;
> If you can trust yourself when all men doubt you, But make allowance for their doubting too:
> If you can wait and not be tired by waiting,
> Or, being lied about, don't deal in lies,
> Or being hated don't give way to hating,
> And yet don't look too good, nor talk too wise…"

Let's not kid ourselves, our youth are in a battle that could result in their death. History has shown that police will kill. Again, the point of this book is not to make a distinction between justifiable or not justifiable; I am simply stating the facts. Police are trained and armed to use whatever force they deem necessary at that moment. Let's not give them a reason to kill or harm us. Let's behave in a way that completely disarms the power structure. We must assist the officer in feeling at ease, safe, and in control in order for us all to make it *home alive*.

Home Alive tip #4: *During a police stop, it is better to be quiet and alive than to speak what is right.*

CHAPTER FOUR 47

Rule #5: Obey the officer.

"Always remember you cannot make a police officer pay for their misconduct at the time that it happens."
—Eric C. Boyles and Adrian O. Jackson, Encounters with Police: A Black Man's Guide to Survival

Before I develop this rule, let me say clearly, up front, and unequivocally that this is the most important rule. Note that the rule is not "Agree with the officer." And I am making no assumptions about whether what the officer is telling you to do is right or wrong. I am very clearly saying: Obey the officer. Given that most police departments are moving towards electronic video and most have recordings, it is increasingly unlikely that they will be telling you to do anything that is going to harm you.

As fellow citizens, we should understand that at the end of the day, the officer, like us, has a strong personal interest in making it home safely. I highlight that because we as law-abiding civilians may be inclined to forget that the vast majority of well-intentioned officers have a certain level of trepidation during citizen-police encounters until they are given reason to feel safe. Typically, the highest level of fear is during the initial moments of the interaction. It's best to try to ease the emotion and lower the inherent intensity of the situation from the outset by showing the officer that you are giving him/her all the power by obeying all commands.

Multiple-choice quiz question: What is the goal of an encounter with the police?

(a) To be respected.
(b) To make it *home alive* and safe.

If you chose (b), you are correct; (a) would be nice, but (b) is the answer. The goal is to make it **home alive and safe!**

In his 1943 paper, "A Theory of Human Motivation," psychologist Abraham Maslow developed what has become known as Maslow's hierarchy of needs. In basic terms, the hierarchy goes like this: to survive and flourish, we all have basic needs. In progressive order, beginning with the most fundamental, these needs are: (1) physiological needs; (2) safety; (3) love/belonging; (4) esteem; and finally (5) self-actualization. Once the physiological needs (air, water, food, etc.) are met, we move on to the next level, safety, and so on up the pyramid. At the top of the pyramid is self-actualization (Janet A. Simons, 1987). Usually you don't skip to a higher stage without first securing the stage below it. If you do not make it past the safety stage, the love/belonging, esteem, and self-actualization stages will matter little to you.

My point? Officers, like all humans, need to feel safe. In their book, *Pulled Over: How Police Stops Define Race and Citizenship,* authors Charles Epp, Steven Maynard-Moody, and Donald Haider-Markel write, "The officer seeks to stay in control, maintain his or her authority, and impose a sanction; the driver seeks to escape with as little punishment and loss of dignity as possible" (Epp, 2014). Because the police officer's fundamental human need of safety is at stake, I am arguing that the civilian's possible loss of dignity is not the officer's greatest concern. Therefore, in your best interest to make the officer's feeling of safety your highest priority, even if that means ridding yourself of concern for your own dignity. Focus on what you must do and need to do get out of the situation physically unharmed and alive. If you don't make it past safety, the remaining levels, i.e., self-esteem, of Maslow's hierarchy of needs will be completely irrelevant to you because you will be dead.

If it is raining and the officer tells you to get on your knees, get on your knees. If it is cold and snowy and the officer asks you to step out the car, then immediately and kindly oblige the officer and step out of the car. If the officer rudely tells you to be quiet, then be quiet. If the officer refers to you in derogatory way, uses a racial or ethnic epithet, or calls you a name, then you be quiet.

You must address the officer in a respectful manner during the encounter, no matter how the officer behaves. In other words, if the officer is acting poorly, you still must treat him or her like king or queen of your world—at that moment and at that time they essentially are. Yes, it is that simple. The officer must feel safe and respected.

I get it. You don't feel safe and respected at that time, so why would you want to make them feel that way? Because you have no power and you must make it *home alive*. It may sound callous, but life is not fair. It is what it is. Hence, you have to be the person who makes the officer feel safe and respected, no matter what.

Let me address two objections people are likely to have to the "Obey the officer" rule. The first goes something like, "Is this dude, the author, telling to me to let the officer treat me like a punk, a 'girl,' a 'sissy,' a sucker, a Joe, a 'bit%#'? Dude is tripping. I am not going out like a punk. He is a doctor; he does not have to deal with what we have to deal with." My answer, let's just say I have not been immune to racial injustice asserted by the police. Racial hate often stokes injustice evenly, regardless of socio-economic status or age. It does not matter who you are, what you do, or how you are dressed. People do not just one wake up one day as whatever their occupation may be. Often people only see color, just ask President Obama.

But, yes, I am absolutely advising you to out-maneuver and out-skill the officer by letting him think he is punking you. Since you've known the encounter with the police is coming one day, you would be a fool if you let the officer goad you into not obeying his commands. This is what we have had to do for decades, outwit and outsmart others.

The second objection is probably something like, "I don't live in that type of area or neighborhood. None of this will happen to me or my loved ones." However, in every single socio-economic demographic, there are people who are not criminals who have been killed by police. Yes, some demographics are impacted more than others, but every interaction with an officer is potentially deadly—and very much more so if the officer does not feel safe and respected.

Let me tell you an ED story that might add some perspective. I'll point out in advance that in many ways physicians have similar charges as police: Treat everyone fairly, don't see color, race, religion, or socio-economics, and be available to help.

The cold truth is, in this world, stuff happens, "BS" happens, things happen, things go wrong. Don't put yourself in a situation or aid in creating an environment where you could be maimed or killed. Obey the officer immediately.

CHAPTER FOUR

As William Shakespeare writes in his play *As You Like It*, "All the world's a stage, and all the men and women merely players; they have their exits and their entrances, and one man in his time plays many parts ..." Play the part you need to play.

We will discuss this further when we get to the chapter specifically written for black males, but as black males, not only do you have to play your part on stage, you must wear the mask, as well. We have to wear the mask that hides our pain. We often have to wear the mask that hides our anger, tears, and contempt for the unjust treatment that we experience in front of our very eyes. Paul Laurence Dunbar, in his poem "We Wear the Mask," sums it up best:

> We wear the mask that grins and lies,
> It hides our cheeks and shades our eyes,—
> This debt we pay to human guile;
> With torn and bleeding hearts we smile, And mouth with myriad subtleties.
>
> Why should the world be over-wise, In counting all our tears and sighs? Nay, lay let them only see us, while We wear the mask.
>
> We smile, but, O great Christ, our cries
> To thee from tortured souls arise. We sing, but oh the clay is vile Beneath our feet, and long the mile; But let the world dream otherwise, We wear the mask!

***Home Alive tip #5**: Officers must feel respected.*

Rule #6: Make the officer feel safe—"Pre-de-escalate."

Safety is a matter of life or death. Choose life.

As I looked up, the officer was reaching for her gun. I started screaming in fear and anger. As the officer pulled her gun out and came closer to the car, she realized I was simply on my phone. But what was clear, she prepared to kill me.

Let me start at the beginning. It was a regular work morning. I woke up, got dressed, made the family breakfast, and kissed my wife and kids goodbye, and left to go to work. As I pulled my car out of my neighborhood, I saw a police vehicle with two officers in the front approaching from the opposite direction, but I did not make much of it.

Within minutes, I looked in the rear-view mirror and saw that the officers had turned their car around and were following me with their lights flashing; they wanted me to pull over. I slowly pulled over. I was used to being pulled over—sometimes deservedly so, sometimes not—so I did not feel a lot of anxiety. After all, I was in my hometown, a mile from my house, and I had done nothing wrong.

The initial part of the stop was fairly routine. Two officers got out of the police car, a young black cleancut male and an older white female. We exchanged pleasantries, and they let me know why I was pulled over, "The front license plate on your car is missing. There has been a rash of people stealing license plates, and attaching them to different cars, and using those in crimes." I apologized and let them know I was unaware that it was missing and that I would correct it right away. The officers took my license and registration and went back to their car.

CHAPTER FOUR

It was rush hour, and I was close to my house and did not want anyone to recognize me and later ask me why I was pulled over. Hence, I reclined my seat to make myself less visible to passing cars and started to do work on my Blackberry while I waited for the officers to run my license through their database.

That is when I looked up and saw the female officer with her gun drawn standing next to my window. Then a new, third officer, a white man, suddenly opened the passenger side door and very coldly and disrespectfully said, "What is the problem? ... there is going to be trouble." I had no idea where he'd come from.

I panicked and started screaming, "What are you doing? Why are you all trying to kill me? Help me!" It was a frightened and anguish-filled scream, not a belligerent one. I kept asking, "Why are you trying to kill me?" This was about a dozen years ago. Clearly, I had not yet absorbed the principles I am setting down in this book. I honestly thought the officers were about to kill me.

For some reason, the big white aggressive male officer who had opened my door abruptly said, "There ain't nothing here," and walked away.

I calmed down—at least I stopped yelling. The officer on the driver's side re-holstered her weapon. She then explained that when I put my seat down, they could no longer see me. I guess they thought that I was attempting to conceal myself from *them* (I wasn't) and that I was, therefore, an imminent threat whom they needed to consider killing.

I went home and wrote letters to my councilman, chief of police, local and state congressman, pastor, and several different people about the incident—I will come back to the letter writing after an incident later in the book.

What is clear to me now, after all the research I've done for this book, including conversations with numerous police officers, is that many officers are scared. The fear is not always present, but when it is, it is real. The officer who drew her gun on me was afraid. It is very important to our own survival that we as civilians recognize this fear. Most, if not all, officers are taught directly or indirectly that their main goal at the end of their shift is to make it home alive. Understandably, officers regularly experience the fear that they may not make it home to their loved ones alive. As a result, they have learned to do whatever they have to do to survive. This may include killing you.

Let's lean further in. If officers are more likely to kill if they are in fear, then our immediate goal is to make an officer feel safe and less fearful. We must "pre-de-escalate" the situation. In other words, before the officer even approaches us, we must take steps to give them no reason to feel anxious or scared. For our own survival, we must endeavor to create the most calming possible situation for the officer.

The following guidelines are not necessarily designed to make you comfortable, respected, or powerful. They are designed to make the officer feel that way, so that you in turn can make it home alive. Again, the goal of the book is to teach us how to make it home alive.

Before the officer even approaches the car:
- Turn the engine off.
- Do not get out of the car unless directed by an officer.
- If it is dark outside, turn on your car's inside light.
- If you have tinted windows, roll all the windows down so that the officer can see inside.

CHAPTER FOUR   55

- Tell all your passengers to keep their hands where the officer can see them.
- Drop or put down whatever is in your hands.

Once you are speaking to an officer during any type of stop:

- Only speak with your mouth. Do not use hand gestures, because officers are trained to see any hand movement as a potential threat.
- Ask the officer, "Is there is anything I can do to make you feel safer?"
- Every time the officer asks you to do something, repeat the question back to the officer, ask for permission to do whatever has been asked of you, then slowly and carefully do it.
- Do not be offended if the officer shines the light directly into your eyes. They are doing this to make it harder for you to see, in case you are intending to take any action to harm them.
- If the officer issues a ticket, sign it. Signing a ticket is not an admission of guilt.
- While you have the right to ask for a supervisor, doing so leaves you in the presence of the officer while you are both waiting for the supervisor to arrive. This could lead to more tickets.
- Complete your encounter with the officer as soon as possible.

I told my son, "No matter what they do, say, or make you feel during the stop, Daddy promises you I can fix you when you get home. But if you are dead, there is nothing I can do and I then have to live in severe pain for the rest of my life".

The entire goal of this book is to arm our youth with additional tools to make it home alive. Brief eye contact only has stirred controversy. The goal is simple – make it home alive. Do what you have to do, be who you need to be, say what you need to say to achieve that objective – complain later.

Brief Eye Contact Only.

This book is for civilians. Yet we must keep in mind that officers have egos like everyone else. Hence, we do not want to do anything that will cause their egos to feel threatened. This includes staring them down.

We have always been taught the eyes are a window to our soul. I agree. But it depends on who is viewing the window. An officer who is hard-hearted, callous, indifferent, or just plain anxious may interpret your respectful look in their eyes as confrontational. And then again, some officers may just start off the encounter afraid and thus be more prone to interpret innocent looks negatively.

Why leave how you look at an officer open to interpretation? History suggests that a youth's respectful and professional look into the eyes of an officer is too often interpreted unfavorably. Look away.

Many of you are thinking that we have been taught and trained to look people in the eye and that we have the right to look people into the eye. I agree. But we are in a struggle to keep our youth alive, and desperate times call for desperate measures. The rules are different for our kids when they are interacting with police. Due to negative media and ingrained stereotypes, many of our youth are prejudged and treated differently. We can't continue to teach them that the world treats them fairly. This sets them up for failure. Again, we are not here to cast moral judgment and philosophize about how things should be. We have to deal with the realities of

CHAPTER FOUR

how things are. We have to train our kids to survive their police encounter. Let's not forget the end game: Make it home alive and unharmed.

In discussing this rule, we must again address the fact that youth are prone to say, "I am a man just like them," or "I am a woman just like them." In stressful situations, this thinking often progresses to loud verbal assertions, such as, "I am a grown #@% man/woman. I can do or say what I want to. I can look the officer in the eye any way I choose to." All of this may be a natural reaction if the young person feels disrespected. But it is also misplaced bravado, and we should not allow it to be perpetuated. We must disabuse ourselves of this type of thinking. The situation has nothing to do with manhood or womanhood. In fact, I have learned that when a youth asserts, "I am a grown woman or man," they are often doing so in an attempt to hide their fear. At the core is really a sense of powerlessness, which leads to a need to prove themselves not only to others, but to themselves. The raw feeling of powerlessness can incite the ego of a young person into confrontation with the police.

Again, it is necessary to explain to your child that they have no power at the moment they are dealing with the police. No, I did not say the child is powerless overall. But on that day, at that moment, during that interaction, the youth is powerless. The officer has all the power. The officer has the right to kill the youth. The youth's power comes from leaving the interaction with the police at that moment, on that day, unharmed and preferably not under arrest. Remember, being arrested by the police does not necessarily mean the youth has committed a crime, but it will significantly decrease the likelihood of being arrested if a young person does not attempt to assert power he does not have in that situation.

Back to the eyes. Often police stops are initiated because a "stare-down" has taken place between the officer and the youth. And if a police officer has already initiated a stop, a stare-down will likely escalate the tension. Is staring at an officer a crime? No, it is not. But it is likely to instigate an unfavorable subjective reaction in the officer and lead the officer to interpret the youth's demeanor and actions in a negative light, and this is an interpretation that we do not want. By the way, you will never hear an officer state for the record, "I did not like how he/she was looking at me," or "He/she was challenging me with his or her eyes." Why? It seems too prejudiced and almost childish. But many officers admit in private that it is often the perceived disrespect of the stare- down that leads down a bad track.

Not only must a youth not initiate a stare-down, but if the officer initiates the stare-down, the youth must also restrain himself from staring back. I have been in situations where an officer has purposely baited me. I have experienced that look of, "I dare you to say or do something. Who do you think you are?" This is a disrespectful look. I know, some say it is hard to interpret a look. But those of us who have experienced those looks from officers know that our interpretation is dead on. We also know that behind that look is "Give me a reason to whip your tail, and I will."

But again, our goal is to make it home alive. Our youth are the ones who have to keep their wits about them and keep their cool, even when the officer is not doing so. They have to be committed to not having a negative interaction with the police, no matter what—

even if the officer is truly in the wrong. Yes, this means being vigilant about how you even look at an officer. I know it sounds strange, but we can't quit. We have to keep on fighting to make sure we leave that interaction alive and unharmed at all costs. We must not give up on staying alive. This reminds me of pieces of a poem called "Don't Quit," which was written by Edgar A. Guest in the early 20th century.

> "When things go wrong, as they sometimes will, When the road you are trudging seems all uphill, When the funds are low and the debts are high, And you want to smile but you have to sigh, When care is pressing you down a bit—
> Rest if you must, but don't you quit . . .
>
> Success is failure turned inside out— The silver tint of the clouds of doubt,
> And you never can tell how close you are—
> It may be near when it seems afar;
> So stick to the fight when you're hardest hit—
> It's when things seem worst that you must not quit."

Home Alive tip #6: *Be aware of the stare trap. Don't look down, but only make brief eye contact.*

Rule #7: No sudden movements and keep your hands out of your pockets.

"It is going to be hard, but hard is not impossible."

It is natural to want to appear to be relaxed even when you are not, especially in a tense situation with the police. One way we instinctively try to appear relaxed is to put our hands in our pockets. For reasons I will explain below, this is a very bad idea when in an encounter with police. Also essential for your health and safety:

- Do not make any sudden movements.
- Do not reach for your cell phone.
- Keep your hands up and out until the officer tells you to put them down.
- Do not lean on anything.
- Do not reach for or into anything.
- Do not even breathe too fast.
- If you have to go to the bathroom, either ask or go in your clothes.

According to the British newspaper *The Guardian*, which keeps a database of US police killings, common reasons given by police when they shoot and kill an American include: "I was in fear for my life," and "I thought they were reaching for something," or "I thought they had a weapon." This is why it is of paramount importance that you do not make any sudden movements.

Even if the officer asks you do something as simple as reach for your wallet, *before* you do, repeat the request back to the officer and wait for an answer. In other words, say something like, "You said it was okay for me to reach for my wallet. I am about to reach for my wallet, okay?" And wait for an answer from the officer or officers. And if the answer is yes, then move very slowly.

I am drawing no inferences and casting no aspersions regarding why the police often think the victim was reaching for a gun. I believe that sometimes the police really thought the victim was reaching for a gun. In many cases, the police, our human partners, were scared and stressed. We have learned that stress causes people's cortisol levels to rise, and that cortisol clouds judgment. In order to avoid a situation in which a scared, stressed officer with cloudy judgment is having to make a life-or-death decision about *you*, don't reach for anything!

Home Alive tip #7: *You move, you lose, you die.*

Rule #8: Start crying.

"Crying is not a sign of weakness. It's a sign of having tried too hard to be strong for too long."

Yes, this may seem strange, but there is a benefit to both parties. From the police perspective, it humanizes the youth; it creates an avenue for understanding and compassion. Tears are often associated with someone who is hurting or someone in need.

Tears are not white or black. Tears are salty. They taste salty. We all have shed and tasted those salty tears when we were children and during difficult moments in our lives. When a young person cries in an encounter with a police officer, the tears are likely to do two things. First, they bind the officer to his or her common human experience with the youth. Second, on a very basic raw emotional level, tears will encourage the officer to experience the youth as the child they still are in many ways, or recently were. We want the officer to view the person as being childlike—children are less intimidating. And if the youth does not otherwise give the impression of being a child, we want the officer to be bombarded with feelings and associations they would have in relation to a child—someone who is innocent and in need of help and compassion.

I know the above has made many blacks cringe, as it does me. Police and Southern whites historically have often treated—and in some areas still treat—fully grown blacks like they were children and have not acknowledged the rights and respect that come with being an adult. That is why many consider calling a black man "boy" to be a racial epithet. And it is. Nevertheless, during stops by the police, we must stay laser focused on the

CHAPTER FOUR 63

goal of this book—arm our youth with strategies to make it home safely. While it personally pains me to say this, for now we have to do what we have to do to survive and make it home from an encounter with the police, so be it. It is not about our feelings. It is about the facts. The facts are – boys are being killed at alarming rates.

Right after graduating from residency, I was working at a community hospital. It was a busy night. The ambulance brought in a 23-year-old male patient who was physically combative and very abusive. Let's call him Thaddaeus. Based on his clothing and the EMS pick-up location, Thaddaeus appeared to be a homeless young drug addict. He was also intoxicated with alcohol. His profile and behavior were not uncommon in the area where this hospital was located.

I proceeded to do a history and physical. Thaddaeus was not cooperative. He kept yelling and cursing. Thaddaeus, who was white, kept calling the medical staff all different types of racial and ethnic epithets. For some reason, he was really locked on the "N" word and kept calling all the black employees the "N" word.

I completed my evaluation and then sedated Thaddaeus. The police soon arrived from the scene where EMS had picked him up. They were unable to interview Thaddaeus because he was too sedated. They asked for us to call them when Thaddaeus woke up because they believed he had been involved in a crime.

Thaddaeus slept for hours. He urinated on himself once so we placed a Foley catheter (plastic tube that goes up his penis to his bladder to constantly drain urine) in him.

Hours later, Thaddaeus woke up more sober, but he was still agitated and verbally abusive. I started to evaluate him more, but had to insist that he stop using the "N" word. And in good drunk fashion, he said, "I don't mean anything by it, I just like to use the word, but man I will stop." Then, out of the blue, he suddenly started crying uncontrollably like a baby. I thought, "Who has time for this? I have patients to see." But he was crying so much I decided to slow down and listen. He shared that he was a full-time student at a local four-year university. He went on to explain that his girlfriend had broken up with him, his parents were getting a divorce, and he was failing out of school. And he confessed to having been on a four-day drinking binge.

Thaddaeus gave me his parents' number, and I confirmed his story. They had been extremely worried and had been looking for him for over a week. Thaddaeus continued to sober up. In general, police do not leave the bedside of a patient who is wanted for a serious crime. Because the police had left his bedside, I assumed that whatever Thaddaeus may have been involved in was minor, and I discharged him as soon as his parents arrived, before the police returned.

The point is, it was not until Thaddaeus started crying that I was able to slow down with a human pause. Even after his use of several offensive racial slurs, Thaddaeus's crying enabled me to see him through a different lens. He was no longer hidden in my plain view. His non-medical humanity was no longer invisible. This reminds me of what Ralph Ellison wrote in his novel *Invisible Man*:

> "I am invisible, understand, simply because people refuse to see me. Like the bodiless heads you see sometimes in circus sideshows,

it is as though I have been surrounded by mirrors of hard, distorting glass. When they approach me, they see only my surroundings, themselves or figments of their imagination, indeed, everything and anything except me" (Ellison, 1952).

The crying attached Thaddaeus to my heart—he was "no longer invisible." It softened me more toward him and made me go beyond my obligations as a physician.

To the unhardened heart, crying presents the opportunity for all parties to view one another in an intimate, selfless way, even if just for one moment. All we need is a moment. The fruit of that moment may very well save a life.

Home Alive tip #8: *Your tears may save your life.*

Rule #9: Do not resist the officer(s).

"The intensity of the pain depends on the degree of resistance to the present moment."
Eckhart Tolle

If the officer decides to take you into custody, do not resist arrest and do not say a word once placed in handcuffs. In March of 1963, Ernesto Miranda was charged with the abduction and rape of an 18-year-old woman in Arizona. While in police custody, Miranda admitted to the crimes. Miranda's attorney argued that his client had not been informed of his rights. The case went all the way to the Supreme Court, and Miranda's conviction was overturned. As a result of the case, police are now obligated to inform every person in custody of their right to remain silent. This mandated warning has become known as the Miranda warning, or Miranda rights (Miranda Warning, 2016).

More than at any other time in your life, the time when you are under arrest is the time to be quiet. If you are prone to lose control and thus need to assert your right to talk, then you are dancing with the devil and do so at your own peril. Here is a complete Miranda warning:

- You have the right to remain silent and refuse to answer questions.
- Anything you say may be used against you in a court of law.
- You have the right to consult an attorney before speaking to the police and to have an attorney present during questioning now or in the future.

CHAPTER FOUR

- If you cannot afford an attorney, one will be appointed for you before any questioning if you wish.
- If you decide to answer questions now without an attorney present, you will still have the right to stop answering at any time until you talk to an attorney.
- Knowing and understanding your rights as I have explained them to you, are you willing to answer my questions without an attorney present (Miranda Warning, 2016)?

In short, what this means is that if you talk to officers all by yourself, anything and everything you say can be interpreted by the officers in a way that helps support the case against you. If you choose to give the legal system the power of interpreting your words, then you are a fool. You are already in police custody, which means in the officer's mind, you are already likely to be perceived as a criminal. The moral arc of understanding is usually not bent favorably toward the perceived criminal.

Implicit in the Supreme Court's decision in Miranda is the acknowledgment that arrestees are likely to feel coerced and anything they say is likely to be interpreted unfavorably by police officers and prosecutors. That is why in our ever-changing legal system all arrestees have the right to consult an attorney and the right to have an attorney present every time they speak to the police. And that is why even if you cannot afford an attorney, "one will be appointed for you before any questioning if you wish." The Supreme Court has given the accused every opportunity not to speak without counsel when talking to the police (Miranda Warning, 2016).

The Supreme Court got it right. Do not talk to the police without counsel.

One more important point. If you are arrested, invoking your Miranda rights does not protect anything you said before you were arrested. If you have not been arrested, anything you say can be used as a reason to put you under arrest. In other words, before, during, and after an arrest, it's better to keep your mouth shut as much as possible.

If you are arrested, it becomes even more important to remain respectful and deferential and recognize that you do not have power over the officers. You are now in full survival mode. They physically have complete control over you, and even though you are technically not a criminal unless a guilty verdict is reached in your case, many officers will consider you to be a criminal once they arrest you. Again, we have to go back to our original theme, even and especially if you are under arrest: Make it **home alive**.

Home Alive tip #9: *"Silence is the source of great strength." —Lao Tzu*

CHAPTER FOUR

Rule #10: When pulled over in a car, everyone in the car is pulled over.

"No man is an island unto himself..."
John Donne

We forget that when anyone is pulled over for a traffic stop by the police, it means that everyone in the car is pulled over, too. That means everyone in the car should follow all the other rules enumerated here, along with the following set of rules that are particular to a traffic stop:

1. As soon as you see the police lights, put your hazard lights on and slow down while you pull over to a safe area.
2. Put the car in park and turn the engine off before the officer even approaches your car. If it is dark, turn on the interior light.
3. If your cell phone is close, turn the volume down and call someone who can hear what is happening. Even if no one answers, the voice mail should record the conversation.
4. As soon as the officer approaches the car, if there are other people in the car let him or her know that there are other people in the car.
5. Let the officer do most of the talking.
6. Do not reach for anything without asking for permission. This includes your license and registration.
7. If asked to exit the car, begin by asking to unbuckle your seatbelt. Then unbuckle it, and proceed *slowly* to get out of the car.

If the officer asks to search your car, and you are innocent, your answer is a judgment call. If you are guilty or have contraband, the answer is a no-brainer: No. But if you are innocent and you consent to having your car searched, you will be putting your trust in the police. It is your constitutional right to refuse a search of your car. I do not recommend consenting to a search of your car.

Jay-Z, in his 2003 song "99 Problems," makes the following observation about a real-life stop by the police when he was younger:

"Well do you mind if I look around the car a bit?"

Well my glove compartment is locked so is the trunk and the back.

And I know my rights so you gon' need a warrant for that.

"Aren't you sharp as a tack? You some type of lawyer or something?

Somebody important or something?"

Child, I ain't passed the bar but I know a little bit

Enough that you won't illegally search my sh%$" (Jay-Z, 2003).

Had Jay-Z consented to a search, his life would be dramatically different now. This song was studied by many legal scholars.

Home Alive tip #10: *Survive today so that you can thrive tomorrow.*

Rule #11: Be a superhero.

"All the best heroes are ordinary people who make themselves extraordinary."

Gerard Way

I have noticed that in many of the interactions between civilians and police that have resulted in a civilian's death, there was a family member present. This is important because in his or her own household, the victim was likely viewed with great admiration and respect, almost as if they were a superhero. And if the person has a son or daughter present, he is probably going to feel the need to maintain that superhero status. Hence, having family members or loved ones present during an encounter with the police often leads a person to try to maintain his dignity and his honor, which can often be a recipe for harm.

Most men, young and old, are accustomed to be being treated with deference and great admiration by their family members, and especially wish to be treated that way by other people in front of their family members. This is a cross-cultural truth. When a male of any nationality or religious background is in the presence of his family, he will want you to treat him with a higher level of respect. Many physicians understand this and treat their patients accordingly. One-on-one, the physician may call the patient by their first name if that is the relationship that has developed. But in the presence of a family member, the doctor is more likely to choose "Mr." or "Mrs." Judges are known to treat a defendant more formally if there are any family members present in the courtroom. Teachers treat students more formally in front of parents. And so on.

The point is, there are unspoken cultural norms that are already in place and established before the officer even engages with the citizen. And if for whatever reason the officer treats the citizen in a disrespectful manner in front of family members, it heightens the tension of the situation.

For example, if a man driving with his family is pulled over by an officer, and the officer approaches the car and immediately starts to shout or mistreat the driver in front of his family, the driver is most likely going to react negatively. The driver's first and innate reaction will be to defend himself and his family against the perceived slight—yes, not just himself, but his family, too, because he is concerned that if the behavior toward him is not stopped, it will spill over and be directed at his family.

For many a man, to be disrespected or minimized in front of his family without pushing back is not acceptable. After all, he has kids, mothers, brothers, and sisters who he is setting an example for. Their feelings of safety and stability are uniquely connected and intertwined with his. If he is the boulder of the family and he is crushed, where does that leave the smaller rocks of the family? There is security in the boulder that would evaporate if the boulder were crushed. The family would be left feeling vulnerable.

Some of you may be thinking, "But it is the *police*. Just smile and bear it." Some men are able to do this, but many are disinclined or unwilling to. This is especially true if the person has had other negative encounters with the police.

The thinking is something like this: I don't like it, I resent it and am infuriated but have to deal with and accept how you treat me when I am by myself. But

CHAPTER FOUR

I'll be damned if I accept you treating me this way in front of my family. This understandable rationale can lead to death during this well- documented crisis our country is facing.

Hence, we have to better prepare our loved ones. The way we do this is to ask men to prepare their families. Particularly if you are the man of the house—and even if you are the woman of the house—share with your family in advance that if you ever get approached or pulled over by the police, you are going to act differently. If the police display any unacceptable behavior, you are simply going to be tolerant of it and will address it at a later time.

Train your kids regularly that this is how Daddy is going to act if he is ever pulled over or approached by the police. Tell them, "Daddy is going to be purposefully meek, humble, and deferential because Daddy wants to be sure that he has a long life with you."

Preparing your family takes the sting out of the need for you to defend your ego and status within the family at the moment of the encounter with the police. What you have basically told them is, "Hey, an unreasonable police officer may speak to me disrespectfully, but I am going to be the bigger and stronger person and let it go for the time being." You will have already explained that you are being strategic, not weak. You are showing your power by allowing the officer to think that you are accepting his/her poor behavior. You are simply doing what is required to make it *home alive* and safe.

If you have experienced treatment by one or more police officers that was in any way illegal or abusive, and your family was present, you must include them in the process of addressing the officers' actions.

Meaning, take them with you when you go to the police station to file your written complaint. Let them help you write you the letter to the local government officials who were elected to help you. Let them see you take appropriate legal action so you can teach them how to deal with inappropriate behavior.

Superheroes have unusual mental, emotional, and physical strength. You must show the very supernatural powers that your family and loved ones have bestowed on you. Be strong and stay quiet and calm. Have tough and robust emotional depth such that even taunts don't bother you. The officer may seek to demean or humiliate you. But you, as a superhero, are expected and must absorb the injustice in the name of staying alive.

There is a good chance that your family members—especially your kids—will have their own ideas about how they would have handled the situation. But they are not the superhero. You are. When you have superhero status, you have been given much. And to whom much is given, much will be expected. You are the standard bearer. Now set the standard.

Home Alive tip #11: **Superheroes** *are able to transform and be whoever they need to be to keep their family safe and to be there for their family.*

Bonus Rule: Stay in your car if at all possible.

"This awareness of the possibility of error sometimes paralyzes all action, it is not to be wondered at that men spend much time and effort to devise means of reducing the possibilities of error."
—**Howard Thurman, Disciplines of the Spirit**

During the research phase of the second edition of this book, I noticed something very concerning. Based on a preponderance of available video, including police dash cam and citizen videos, I noticed that the danger for a citizen seems to increase when the citizen gets out of their car during a traffic stop. Yes, I am aware that many states believe it is safer for the officer when the citizen is out of the car. But I am not sure how safe it is for the citizen.

To be clear: an officer has the legal right to ask you to exit your vehicle during a traffic stop, even for something as minor as forgetting to use your turn signal when changing lanes. This legal authority was granted to police in the 1977 Supreme Court case of Pennsylvania v. Mimms. However, it is in your best interest and the officer's to have a physical barrier between you. Staying in the car maintains that barrier. When there is no physical barrier, the officer's anxiety is likely to increase.

At the end of the day, officers do what they think they have to do to protect themselves from perceived danger.

This means we have to do everything we can to avoid any situation that makes the officer feel unsafe. Under circumstances where all parties are apprehensive, like a police traffic stop, each additional choice that is added to the mix introduces the possibility of error. We want to minimize the number of actions we initiate, which will minimize the number of choices the officer has to make, and thus the number of possible errors they can make. The more that fear is part of the decision-making process, the higher the risk of error. So, again, we do not want to do anything that will cause the officer to feel unsafe.

Remember that all people, including police officers, tend to see what they expect to see. If the officer is expecting to see aggressive behavior or a life-threatening movement, that is what the officer is going to see, even if there is no aggressive behavior.

Unfortunately, like all humans, officers enter situations with their own implicit bias. Simply put, implicit bias refers to the attitudes, thoughts, and views that affect one's understanding or interpretation of a matter in ways one that not be fully conscious.

Hence, whatever biases the officer has concerning you are going to be reflected in how they interact with you. The implicit biases associated primarily with black males and other young males are not likely to be favorable. Hence, it is vitally important that you do everything you can to keep from having to suddenly interact with an officer and his/her biases.

According to multiple sources, the top five reasons police officers stop citizens:

1. Speeding
2. Cell phone use
3. Equipment modifications and violations (e.g., tinted windows)
4. Not wearing a seatbelt
5. Driving while Black or Hispanic

CHAPTER FOUR 77

(National Institute of Justice).

I will address reason number five below—that one is not in your control. However, speeding, talking on a non-headset phone while driving, and tinting your windows are in your control. And by not doing any of those things you will reduce the likelihood of being pulled over by the police—as you will if you wear a seatbelt.

As for being Black or Hispanic: you—we—cannot change that. We simply must assume we are going to be stopped by police while driving, all the more reason the other rules in this book are of paramount importance to us.

Under no circumstances should you get out of your vehicle without being asked to during a traffic stop. Also, you must do everything in your power to keep the officer from asking you to get out of your car. The main steps you must take to avoid being asked to step out of your vehicle are all steps you should take in advance of being stopped:

- No drinking and driving. This means no driving for at least 12 hours after your last drink.
- Be sure that you have the registration to the car that you are driving and it is current.
- Have a current driver's license with you.
- Make sure that both of your brake lights work.
- Be sure that your headlights work.
- Have proof of insurance in the vehicle—some states require it.
- Be sure that the appropriate license sticker is on the car.
- If there is any significant damage to your car, have it fixed right away. Officers often believe

that if a car's damage has not been fixed, it means the driver does not have insurance.

Parents and care providers, please use the above list as a weekly checklist for your loved one(s).

It could be that you follow all these rules and the officer still asks you to get out of the car—there are no guarantees. So be prepared for that to happen. Remain calm. Move slowly. Keep your hands visible to the officer at all times. Comply with the officer's requests or commands.

At the risk of sounding like a broken record, the goal is to make it home alive. Admittedly, there are a lot of reasons to be disturbed or upset that we even have to discuss these rules. But I humbly remind you that is not the point of this book. The point is to save your life and your children's lives.

The Psychiatric Patient

"You are valuable just because you exist. Not because of what you do or what you have done, but simply because you are,"

—Max Lucado, *No Wonder They Call Him the Savior*

In a 2015 study, researchers at the Treatment Advocacy Center found that the risk of being killed during a police encounter is 16 times greater for individuals with untreated severe mental illness than for other civilians. This constitutes a major public health crisis (Fuller et al., 2015).

Approximately 44 million Americans—or 20 percent of the population—experience mental illness in a given year. And about 10 million of those experience a severe mental illness that disorders their thinking. We know many of these people. We see many of these Americans in our daily lives, and at times we do not even notice their disease. They are often the homeless, the intoxicated, and the "strange" whom many of us treat as invisible.

The researchers write that while fewer than 4 in 100 Americans have a severe mental illness, "individuals with severe mental illness generate no less than 1 in 10 calls for police service and occupy at least 1 in 5 of America's prison and jail beds. An estimated 1 in 3 individuals transported to the hospital emergency rooms in psychiatric crisis are taken there by the police."

The police and the mentally ill encounter each other with great frequency and in multiple ways. This is important, for as the *New York Times has reported,* "having more encounters with police officers, can create a greater risk of a fatal shooting" (Mullainathan, 2015). As the Treatment Advocacy Center report also states, "Individuals with mental illness also make up a disproportionate number of those killed at the very first step of the criminal justice process: while being approached or stopped by law enforcement in the community." The report goes on to say that "a minimum of 1 in 4 fatal police encounters ends the life of an individual with severe mental illness."

The mentally ill are more likely to hurt themselves than they are others. But the reaction by the police suggests that officers are unaware of this fact. Additionally, the severely mentally ill are far less likely than other civilians to be able to adhere to the norms, nuances, and expectations of an encounter with law enforcement, even if they do not pose a threat. Combine that with the fact that many officers and police personnel do not have the appropriate training to manage the acutely mentally ill and you now have the recipe for a disastrous encounter.

For several social reasons, many psychiatric patients, and especially black male patients, do not receive early treatment and thus are more likely to be brought in by police in custody. Hence, alliances with treatment providers are often compromised when patients are brought in against their will. The most important step you can take to help your loved ones with mental illness or signs of mental illness is early treatment and intervention. Evidence shows that the pathway forward is less violent and less bumpy when the patient has established relationships with a provider before their disease process progresses.

Patients who do not have established relationships with a primary psychiatric care provider are more apt to find themselves in dangerous predicaments.

An experience I had in my job as an emergency physician illustrates this problem. It was a busy day in an urban emergency department in Michigan, where I was one of two attending physicians—i.e., physicians in charge.

EMS brought in a patient by ambulance with the complaint of "bizarre behavior" and presented him to the nurse triage station for an initial hospital assessment.

The patient was a 20ish-year-old male with a disheveled appearance. Let's call him Gabriel. During the initial nursing assessment, Gabriel casually and calmly got off the stretcher and started yelling, "They are after me ... I am God ... I want to go to heaven ... I am really scared." He then refused to sit down and started to move toward the exit. Gabriel was clearly exhibiting signs of paranoia with a psychotic component.

CHAPTER FOUR

I was the physician called over to assist. Every time I moved closer to Gabriel, he moved away in fear. I calmly informed him that I was not going to hurt him and he was in safe hands. I asked if he had any medical problems. I also asked if he had done any illegal drugs. Gabriel admitted to doing phencyclidine, known as PCP, a hallucinogenic drug. Gabriel also had a history of bipolar schizophrenia and had not been taking his medications.

I proceeded to try to talk to Gabriel, and he finally agreed to sit down and let the nurse take his blood pressure. While she was taking his blood pressure, Gabriel became very combative and again started shouting at the top of his lungs, "I am God. I will not let you hurt me. I don't want to die, and I will not let you kill me!"

I calmly reminded Gabriel that the entire ED staff was there to help him. He calmed down and sat back down. Then again, but this time more aggressively, he jumped up and said, "I am God, I will save you," and then proceeded to try to walk out. We were able to keep him from walking out, but this time also called the hospital police to assist.

Gabriel became more combative and aggressive. When the police arrived to physically restrain him, a full- fledged brawl ensued. The officers gained control, and I simultaneously ordered and administered an injection of sedative medication in his arm. We placed him in four-point restraints (both arms and both legs) on a stretcher. We placed him on one-to-one observation with an emergency department tech in an open but private room.

A few hours later, I did a full history and physical on Gabriel. He was friendly and very cooperative. He said that he felt like himself again. Clinically, Gabriel appeared normal, with no observable aggressive behavior. Thought content and pattern appeared appropriate. I had his restraints removed and observed Gabriel from afar. He was calm, cooperative, and appropriate. Several minutes later, an emergency tech asked me if it was okay to have the hospital police escort Gabriel to the bathroom so we could get a urine sample. I said okay. And as per protocol for patients who required restraints, we had to get the police to escort the tech with the patient.

About 20 minutes later, the tech came and whispered to me, "I don't think Gabriel is breathing." I immediately went and assessed the patient. He was not breathing and did not have a pulse. We immediately began CPR and initiated advanced cardiac life support protocols, ACLS. We rolled him to the trauma room. I intubated him. We placed an IV and gave him several doses of epinephrine and other lifesaving medicines. We placed him on a cardiac monitor. He was in V-fib (ventricular fibrillation). We shocked him with 200 Joules. No success, then we shocked him with 300 Joules—nothing. Finally, we shocked him with 360 Joules, and he flat-lined (no cardiac activity). We continued CPR and gave him several more rounds of epinephrine, atropine, sodium bicarbonate, and other lifesaving medicines. Nothing worked. After 35 minutes of our lifesaving attempts, Gabriel was pronounced dead at 4:55 a.m.

On further investigation, I learned that when the emergency department tech and police escorted Gabriel to the bathroom, he started talking loudly again. The officers asked him to lower his voice. Gabriel said that he did not have to lower his voice and began to yell at the officers in front of other patients. Gabriel refused to listen to the officers. Gabriel again claimed to be God. One of the officers reportedly said, "You don't seem to understand; I am in charge here, not you. Now do as I told you." Gabriel reportedly refused again. The officers then went to restrain him and a violent fight began. The officers aggressively subdued Mr. Gabriel and placed him back on the stretcher. No one knows if he was still breathing at that point.

Unfortunately, this is a distressing example of how things can go terribly bad fast. The officers felt disrespected when Gabriel began to speak loudly to them and feared for their safety. The officers' and Gabriel's escalating behavior caused the situation to abruptly take a turn for the worse and, within a blink of an eye, a person was dead.

Regardless of the who, what, when, and where, Gabriel's was dead. As I had to inform his family, the cries and screams of Gabriel's mother and the rest of his family were no different from the shrieks of a family whose deceased loved one did not have a mental illness. Again, tears taste salty. We have an American crisis that permeates all areas and aspects of our lives. The psychiatric patients bear the brunt of a large proportion of the problem.

The disproportionate number of mentally ill people who are injured or killed during encounters with police is a crisis-within-the-crisis. In the rest of this book, I am addressing civilians regarding what to do to make it home alive from an encounter with the police. But the mentally ill comprise a special case. As was true of Gabriel, they are often not able to regulate their behavior as I am advising other civilians to do when interacting with law enforcement. Therefore, it is all the more incumbent on the police and those who train them to protect this large and vulnerable segment of the population.

The Psychiatric Patient and Use of Force

As a country, we must create and implement policies that restrict the use of deadly force in all cases, because it is all too likely that officers will arrive at a scene and believe they are apprehending a criminal, when in reality they are seeing a person with a psychiatric ailment who is hallucinating with disorganized thoughts. An officer who does not have the skill set to identify the difference should have extensive training in non-lethal methods of managing civilians who seem to pose a threat—particularly if those civilians are unarmed.

It is vital and urgent that all police departments regularly review, update, and provide ongoing officer training in their use-of-force policies. More poignantly, the use-of-force policies should include specific recommendations about how to identify, how to engage, and when to engage citizens who are experiencing an acute mental health crisis.

Not only is reviewing the use-of-force policies critical, but it is paramount that police officers receive additional and specific training and skills regarding how to identify and interact with psychiatric patients. There are several proven programs available to assist and train police organizations on how to interact with the mentally ill. The most well-known is Crisis Intervention Training (CIT). CIT is a nationally-recognized model for community policing that has proven to save lives when implemented. CIT training consists of a 40-hour course specifically designed for law enforcement and taught by behavioral health specialists. The training includes verbal de-escalation and scenario-based training in crisis response. Find out more at *https://www.nami.org/Law-Enforcement-and-Mental-Health/What-Is-CIT*.

The mentally ill are our neighbors, friends, children, teachers, and colleagues, who are often stabilized by prescription medications—and, as many of us know, that stability can easily be disrupted. They are us, and we are them. The mentally ill are woven into the fabric of American life—their comfort and safety and ours are inextricably linked.

We must all be ready for the day when we, our loved ones, or our fellow citizens experience an acute or an exacerbated mental health crisis. We want them to be alive at the end of that crisis. We need those who are called to assist during this difficult period to be appropriately trained.

As active participants in our communities, we are called to action. Inquire if your local law enforcement organizations are CIT-trained. Ask if the use-of-force policies for your local police agencies have been updated in the past five years. And if not, inquire when it will be done. During a police-initiated stop would not be the time to inquire.

Finally, be sure to vote in every local election for people willing to appoint chiefs of departments who will implement use-of-force policies that adequately protect and serve our loved ones and who will provide the appropriate training for officers to safely do their jobs.

CHAPTER FIVE

BLACK MALES PART 1— TREATED DIFFERENTLY

"The cruel reality is that nothing black people could say or do can change the minds of the white people who believe that black folks are a threat to them. They will neither love the blacks nor leave them alone. Black people cannot be smart enough, good enough, or humble enough to please those who despise them, especially when they find legal cover for the animus behind a badge and a gun. Not even the election of a black president could unseat that stubborn fact. The murder of unarmed black motorist Walter Scott by white officer Michael Slager in South Carolina in April 2015 sheds light on political and social realities that surround similar cases of lethal force against black people. Americans have been forced to lower their expectations for racial justice and now measure racial progress in painfully minimal terms. The tragedy also brings into focus the optics of race—how black people are seen on camera and in history, revealing how black life is valued or degraded. And the spectacle of Scott's death highlights the fast terror that stalks black life even as it obscures the slow terror that blacks routinely confront in the Age of Obama." —Michael Eric Dyson, *The Black Presidency: Barack Obama and the Politics of Race in America* (Dyson, 2016).

CHAPTER FIVE

I am writing this chapter and the one that follows for black males for the reasons addressed by Dr. Dyson above and because the statistics with which I began this book clearly show that black people are being killed by police at a rate at least more than two-and-a-half times higher than that of white people. This book is intended for everyone—I want to help keep everyone safe. But when it comes to encounters with the police, black people—and black young men, in particular, are a demographic group who, the facts have clearly shown, are in grave danger. Therefore, they deserve particular attention.

While I have specifically focused on black males in these last two chapters of the book, it is also important to say that black women are at risk, as well. Though the statistics from *The Guardian* show that black males are at greater risk of being killed by police than black females, they also show that black females are more than two times as likely to be killed or assaulted by police as white females.

Additionally, every time a black boy or black man is killed or assaulted by the police, the emotional burden, as well as the economic burden, is borne by the women—women who already are likely to be paid less than their male counterparts.

Legal scholar Kimberlé Crenshaw coined the term "intersectionality." Her argument is basically that if a person fits into more than one demographic that is discriminated against, you have to see that person as an intersection of those categories. Hence, if someone is a woman *and* black, there are two forms of discrimination she is up against—misogyny and racism. In this book, I am focusing on black males because they are more directly at risk of death in encounters with the police. But I now understand that because of this "intersectionality," the killings and violence committed by the police against black woman are underreported or unnoticed by the media and America. Black women are in need of attention, support, and help for equally compelling reasons.

Black females, black males, and the police have historically had a turbulent and deadly past that dates back to slavery and the days of Jim Crow, when the Ku Klux Klan member and the policeman may have been one and the same. It was the police committing violent crimes against the blacks. Variations of discontent, disconnect, and violence exist in America today. Studies show that blacks and especially black males are suspended from school at higher rates than whites for the same infractions. The justice system has consistently given blacks longer and stiffer sentences than their white peers for the same crimes. Blacks are paid less than their white counterparts for doing the same job with the same qualifications. Blacks have higher mortality rates (Frank Sloan, 2010). These are just a few of the glaring disparities, and data does not show significant improvement.

With the 2008 election of President Barack Obama, many naïve people would like to classify America as a race- neutral society. While I appreciate the optimistic outlook, it is misleading and dangerous to black males. America and black males have had a longstanding dysfunctional relationship.

As William Cullen Bryant once said, "Truth crushed to earth will rise again." The truth is the truth, no matter how we clean it up or try to explain it away. The data shows that police have gravely and with impunity mistreated black men for years. Yet, in May of 2017 the House and Senate along with the support of President Trump introduced a bill, Back the Blue Act of 2017. This bill, if passed, would make it virtually impossible for citizens to have any civil recourse for egregious misconduct committed by law enforcement. Hence, when the truth shall "rise again" there will likely not be a punishment.

Either way our American crisis will not be fixed overnight, and it will not be easy. But as the famous motivational speaker Les Brown says, "You do not have to be great to start. But you have to start to be great." As we start, there is a certain amount of foundational knowledge from the 2014-2018 literature that will frame the crisis:

1. "48% of unarmed people killed by the 100 largest city police departments were black. These police departments killed unarmed black people at 4 times higher than unarmed white people."

2. "People have a bias to perceive young black men as bigger (taller, heavier, more muscular) and more physically threatening (stronger, more capable of harm) than young white men" (Racial Bias in Judgement Size and Formidability: From Size to Threat"- *Journal of Personality and Social Psychology,* March 2017).

3. "Rates of violent crime in cities did not make it any more or less likely for police departments to kill people. For example, Buffalo and Newark police departments had low rates of police violence despite high crime rates, while Spokane and Bakersfield had relatively low crime rates and high rates

of police violence" (Mapping Police Violence, 2018).

4. In Chicago, a 2016 Police Accountability Task Force report found that "black and Hispanic drivers were searched approximately four times as often as white drivers, yet [the Chicago Police Department's] own data show that contraband was found on white drivers twice as often as black and Hispanic drivers."

5. "There were 511 officers killed in felonious incidents and 540 offenders from 2004 to 2013, according to FBI reports. Among the total offenders, 52 percent were white, and 43 percent were black" (Lee, 2015).

6. "Although deaths of police officers are well documented, no reliable official US data exists on the number of persons killed by the police, in part because of long-standing and well-documented resistance of police departments to making these data public" (Nancy Krieger, 2015).

America is a great country and will continue to be great. We must continue to bring all under the umbrella of "united we stand." The alternative consequence is "divided we fall." If we have one segment of the population that has been here since America's inception who is suffering disproportionately, we all suffer. It is not until the chain is fully strengthened throughout that we will have fulfilled our true greatness. Black males are not the weak link. But they are being weakened by a system that does not appreciate them as much as they do other groups. Reasons are bilateral and fixable.

This is highlighted in music. I am unabashedly a self- proclaimed hip hop fan. I favor all types of music, but old school hip hop speaks a message of hope to many, and especially to black males. No, I did not say all hip hop. One of my favorite groups is Public Enemy, from the 1980s and 90s. They had a message of hope and understanding, while simultaneously offering a message of warning. Professor Griffith of Public Enemy, deploying his lyrical genius in the group's 1988 album, *It Takes a Nation of Millions to Hold Us Back*, and in the song "Don't Believe the Hype" writes:

> "The minute they see me, fear me
> I am the epitome, a public enemy
> Used, abused without clues
> I refused to blow a fuse
> They even had it on the news
> Don't believe the hype"

Professor Griffith goes on and speaks what he thinks America is thinking: "Again I said I was a time bomb / in the daytime the radio's scared of me / Cause I'm mad, plus I'm the enemy ..." (Public Enemy). In short, if you are black— whether light-, medium- or dark-skinned, with tight or curly hair, a professional athlete, high school dropout, Ph.D., JD, MD, sporting an Armani suit with designer loafers, digging ditches, wearing a hoodie, wearing your pants pulled down to your upper thighs—you are feared. You are still that black man whom many have been taught to fear. Yes, very successful black folk are viewed the same. You are successful, but you are still a black man and thus still viewed through a racial lens that historically has been very hateful and fearful of you. No matter your success or status, you are often viewed through that one lens.

Dr. Dyson underscores this point in his book: "During a recent seven-year stretch, a white officer killed a black person nearly twice a week in America, underscoring the belief among blacks that they are targets of racial profiling and its violent twin, police brutality" (Dyson, 2016). Many outside the black community think that the exercise of lethal force is warranted in most cases involving blacks and the cops. As discussed earlier in this book, police are able to arrest and subdue other minorities with far fewer instances of lethal force, but when it comes to blacks, it appears that a kill is more likely and a de-escalation less so. Watch for the distraction. Many want to change the focus to black-on-black crime, as former New York Mayor Giuliani recently did during a national interview about the rash of police killings. In a discussion of the police killings of Philando Castile and Alton Sterling in July of 2016, the mayor suddenly wanted to pivot and talk about the reported statistic that 94 percent of blacks killed are killed by other blacks. He either did not know or failed to mention that when it comes to murder, 88 percent of whites are killed by whites, as well. Most Hispanics who are murdered are killed by other Hispanics. Boyfriends kill girlfriends. Husbands kill wives. The bottom line is people kill where they live.

It was a sad moment in American politics. Former Mayor Giuliani indicted himself. He was the leader of a city that had greater than 94 percent of murdered blacks being killed by other blacks. He was the mayor of everyone in the city— not everyone except blacks. What did his administration do about the public health issue of blacks being killed? The mayor tacitly admitted to abdicating his responsibility to support and protect all people in the city. Black males were excluded by Mayor Giuliani from the American dream as a result of their blackness.

It would have been appropriate and truthful for him to highlight that it is not just about blacks killing

CHAPTER FIVE

blacks. It is about an environment primed by rules and regulations for the killing of people of color and poor whites.

Ta-Nehisi Coates, discussing the killing of his friend Prince Jones by police officers in his book, *Between the World and Me*, powerfully and succinctly writes:

> "The killing fields ... were created by the policy of Dreamers, but their weight, their shame, rests solely upon those who are dying in them. There is great deception in this. To yell "black-on-black crime" is to shoot a man and then shame him for bleeding. And the premise that allows for these killing fields—the reduction of the black body—is no different than the premise that allowed for the murder of Prince Jones. The Dream of acting white, of talking white, of being white, murdered Prince Jones as sure as it murders black people in Chicago with frightening regularity. Do not accept the lie. Do not drink the poison. The same hands that drew red lines around the life of Prince Jones drew red lines around the ghetto" (Coates, 2015).

In other words, we highlight black-on-black crime. But no one talks about the crimes against blacks that are far more atrocious than black-on-black crime and that create the conditions in which black-on-black crime flourishes. No one talks about the legally planned and created system that supports and creates the environment for the killing of black men. That system allows companies to set up factories that lead to the severe compromise of the environment surrounding black communities. The environment—the air they breathe, the water they drink—is often toxic to the habitants of the local community. Then we see the killing begin long before a youth is even old enough to know what a gun is.

In this case, the environment *is* the gun. The environment is the gun that causes the high rate of infant mortality that the community has no control over. It is the gun that causes a higher death rate among women in low-income areas than elsewhere. The gun is the inundation of underserved communities with liquor stores that sit on so many corners—this simply does not exist in higher-income areas. This gun allows for no stores that sell fresh fruits and vegetables in lower-income areas, but allows for a preponderance of fast food chains and convenience stores.

We all like to talk about the kind of guns that shoot bullets. But nobody talks about the systemic and structural economic and social factors in place that lead to the death of millions before the black male even takes his first breath. You fix the structural and economic problems, and you would cut black-on-black crime by more than 50 percent, by my estimate.

CHAPTER SIX

BLACK MALES PART 2 — IT'S GOING TO BE OKAY

"Live out of your imagination instead of out of your memory."
—Les Brown

We are people. We were all born, and we will all die. We are all created equal by the creator. The world does not treat us equally. Equality is fleeting. Fortunately, we are all given 60 seconds in one minute. Let's be clear, I am not disillusioned by the disparity of resources to help utilize people's 60 seconds. But nevertheless, we all have 60 seconds each minute.

What is not fleeting is the pain that inequality creates. On some level, we are all broken people. But some people are more broken than others. The trials and tribulations of the lives of black males often make us more broken. The harsher life treats you, the more broken you become, unless you are able to learn to forgive and let things go. Not forgiving robs or saps you of needed strength. It keeps you from being able to maximally utilize all of your strength. It leaves you disadvantaged. And it prevents some from moving forward to achieve your maximum potential. As parents, we need to be vigilant, ready, and strong, prepared to maximize all of our energies and strength. We need all of our strength and our potential strength to be ready and fully available.

Our black males need their parents to be encouraged and strengthened soldiers, always ready to teach, train, and protect them. The assault on black males continues and, it could be argued, has increased! We need you, their home base and the source of their strength, to be vigilant and ready, and not mired down by the very real hurts of your past.

As the parents of black youths, we have to do whatever we can to minimize the hurt this society inflicts on us; and when we are hurt, we must do whatever we can to heal ourselves. Otherwise, it will be more difficult to heal the hurts of our young black males, because often hurt people inflict hurt on others. The world is going to perpetually inflict an unjustifiable amount of pain on the minds and bodies of our black males, a kind of agony that their peers do not have to endure and probably cannot imagine. Let's maximize our strength by settling within ourselves the pain of transgressions of our past. In no way am I minimizing pains of the past. It is not within the scope of this book to walk through healing thyself. So we are going to make a few gigantic leaps in the interest of helping our black males. Not forgiving leads to anger. Perpetual anger can lead to bitterness. Bitterness can lead to misery. Miserable people are often not very strong; they are often unproductive and the least emotionally available people. Let's do everything in our power to be emotionally available to our black males.

Most people think the first step toward forgiving is an apology from the perpetrator(s). This is the furthest thing from the truth. Forgiveness is not a feeling or an emotion. Forgiveness is a group of decisions or

CHAPTER SIX

actions that the wronged or offended chooses in order to prevent the offender from continuing to inflict pain long after the actual harmful event is over. Forgiveness does not mean forgetting. But it does mean that we don't allow the infraction to have control over us. As Bishop Desmond Tutu said in *The Book of Forgiving*, "Forgiveness does not relieve someone of responsibility for what they have done. Forgiveness does not erase accountability." But forgiveness acknowledges that to remain in a state of rage toward your perpetrator is akin to drinking poison to kill your enemy. It is the offended person who has to actively move toward forgiveness. In forgiveness, the subsequent actions of the offender after the harming event are irrelevant. More succinctly, the person, people, or system that wronged you need not be active participants in your forgiveness. The decision to forgive others or systems is all within you. But most people don't believe that to be true. However, the difficulty with not believing it, and not forgiving, is that the apology you may wish for and certainly deserve is likely not forthcoming, if it has not already happened.

I know how very hard it is to forgive. I know I may not convince you of the value of forgiveness, and I know many people need an apology for past transgressions in order to forgive. As the official representative of personal, state, and federal apologies, let me now apologize for the wrongs of so many people and systems who have harmed you.

To you, black parent, I sincerely apologize on behalf of all those who should have apologized to you. I apologize for all the times you were judged with bias or prejudged based on the color of your skin. I am sorry that you were the most qualified person, but you did not get the job or the school admission because you were not white. I am sorry for the world making it difficult for you just because it could. I am sorry about the sneers and sighs when you ask a question or need clarification. I am sorry about all of the times you are not given the benefit of the doubt. I am sorry that they talked to you like you were a child, while you were standing there, clearly a full-grown adult. I am sorry that when you buy a house, they charge you a higher interest rate because of your color. I am sorry that you were charged more for your car just because you were black. I am sorry that you were only shown certain neighborhoods by the realtor. I am sorry that laws were passed concerning illegal drugs that clearly targeted you. I am sorry that "the minute they see you, they fear you."

I am sorry that you are constantly over-policed. I am really sorry that, unlike your white male colleagues, you are rarely given the simple "benefit of the doubt."

I am sorry for all those times your mother or grandmother did not protect you from your uncle or neighbor next door. I am sorry that sometimes daddy drank too much and did and said things that were frankly wrong. I am sorry that you had to be home alone so often because I had to work two and three jobs. I am sorry that I missed your game because I had to work. I apologize for the times you had to ride home with people you did not like. I am sorry for not being able to fix you dinner. I am sorry that you had wake up alone and get ready for school alone. I am sorry I was not there to help you with your homework. I am sorry I missed the parent-teacher conference and the teacher had the gall to ask you why I did not show up. I am sorry that I was not there for you to tell me about the bullying. I am sorry that I was not there to help you choose a different path.

Yes, I know you worked at your desk because you did not have money for lunch. I am sorry for all the times you needed someone to step up and protect you from the world and no one was there. I am sorry for all the times you needed the cavalry and no one was there. I am sorry that the world was just mean to you for the sake of being mean.

In short, I apologize on behalf of all those who have harmed and hurt you. I am sorry on behalf of all those who aided and abetted in the creation of your pain. I am sorry for everything wrong that has happened to you. I am sorry that you simply needed the benefit of the doubt and were not granted it and had to deal with the consequences of it not being afforded to you.

Now, it is highly likely that the apologies you received in the preceding paragraphs are the only apologies you will ever receive for past infractions. The interesting part is, many people, particularly white people, are not even aware of how many infractions are directly or unknowingly racially motivated.

I hope you will either be able to forgive others for their trespasses or accept my apology above on their behalf. Either way, one thorny problem remains: The guilt you feel. The hardest person to forgive is ourselves, for tolerating poor treatment. Even if we cannot forgive others, we have to forgive ourselves for our perceived allowance of letting someone treat us poorly. We have to forgive ourselves for believing that we could have protected our loved one more successfully from others and the system. We have to forgive ourselves for being so hard on our own children—for possibly not protecting their natural right to be a child. The truth is you probably tried to protect your loved one just as fiercely as a bear protects her cubs. Don't be too hard on yourself—being superman or superwoman is not easy, and even superman is not always successful.

We have to forgive ourselves for aiding in taking the innocence of our own loved ones. Ta-Nehisi Coates eloquently makes this point in *Between the World and Me*:

> "All my life I'd heard people tell their black boys and black girls to 'be twice as good,' which is to say 'accept half as much.' These words would be spoken with a veneer of religious nobility, as though they evidenced some unspoken quality, some undetected courage, when in fact all they evidenced was the gun to our head and the hand in our pocket. This is how we lose our softness. This is how they steal our right to smile. No one told those little white children, with their tricycles, to be twice as good. I imagined their parents telling them to take twice as much. It seemed to me that our own rules redoubled plunder. It struck me that perhaps the defining feature of being drafted into the black race was the inescapable robbery of time, because the moments we spent readying the mask,
> or readying ourselves to accept half as much, could not be recovered. The robbery of time is not measured in lifespans but in moments. It is the last bottle of wine that you have just uncorked but do not have time to drink. It is the kiss that you do not have time to share, before she walks out of your life. It is the raft of second chances for them, and twenty-three-hour days for us."

Let's stop stealing the softness of our children by

teaching them to be twice as good, which, interpreted to the next degree, means to accept half as much. We should simply teach them excellence. We should not teach our black boys to just do their best—most people do not know what their best is—but teach them to do what is **necessary** to achieve their desired outcome. As it relates to police interactions, the desired outcome is to make it *home alive* and unharmed.

Save their lives.

CONCLUSION

"It's not always easy, but that's life. Be strong. Know that there are better days ahead."

—unknown

Difficult times introduce a person to themselves. Don't allow your spirit to be weakened. Yes, it may be tested, weathered, beaten up, or even hurt, but not weakened. Whatever small or great confidence you possess is yours. It was not given to you by anyone else. So don't let anyone take it. You may need to lick your wounds or even cry for a moment. That is okay. But you can't tap out. You *must* stay in the game of life as a full participant and stake your claim.

I am reminded of a poem I learned and memorized while in college, "Invictus," by William Ernest Henley:

> "Out of the night that covers me, Black as the pit from pole to pole, I thank whatever gods may be
> For my unconquerable soul.
> In the fell clutch of circumstance
>
> I have not winced nor cried aloud. Under the bludgeoning of chance My head is bloody, but unbowed.
>
> Beyond this place of wrath and tears Looms but the Horror of the shade, And yet the menace of the years Finds, and shall find

me, unafraid.

It matters not how strait the gate,
How charged with punishments the scroll, I am the master of my fate:
I am the captain of my soul."

Back to the 60 seconds. I would like to specifically address young people. The only thing we all possess in this world that is equal is time. We all have the same 60 seconds in a minute, the same 60 minutes in an hour, the same 24 hours in a day, the same 365 days in a year, and the same 10 years in a decade. It is what we do with that time that distinguishes us from one another. Let's not start with the decade, or the year, or the day, or the hour. Let's start with 60 seconds. It is what you do with each moment that will determine your path in this world. Each moment prepares you for the next moment. Seize each instant and make it work for the benefit of your life and the life of someone else.

Yeah, I get that life is not fair. Truth is, life is never going to be fair. We have to use our 60 seconds in such a productive way that even when the twin evils of racism and fear of us creep in, our minutes have been used so productively that momentum takes over.

Look at it this way. What if you were given $86,400? And you were allowed to spend it on anything you want? The only rule is you can't carry it over to the next day. What would you do? I am sure you would feel great pressure, joy, motivation and focus to spend the $86,400 – especially knowing that at the end of the day it is gone. View the 86,400$ as time and every day you are alive, you are given 86,400 seconds. The 86,400 seconds is more valuable than money. What are you doing with your 86,400 seconds? Use the seconds with great passion and purpose. Let the world know that you are here. Spend your time motivated and with great purpose. Change the world! You want to be exhausted at the end of the day. You want to end on empty-nothing in the tank! Sleep only as much as your body requires. And then be prepared for your next 86,400 seconds.

Our hours must be filled with the unbending and unyielding spirit of "I am and will become what I choose to become, not what you want me to be." It is an unflinching commitment to your higher power, your God and my Lord and Savior to become the best person you choose to be.

There will be those monumental moments that the decision you make at that time will change your life forever— for good or for bad. On a side note, there are two decisions you must never make: To live a life that does not have a divine entity greater than you at the center and to drop out of high school. And the decision to drop out of school alone makes it 80 percent more likely that life will not be pleasant for you. Additionally, the decision to live without a Godly or celestial source of strength, power, and faith will limit your ability to live a fulfilled life.

Decide wisely. When you have reached the limit of your own insights—and we all reach that limit—seek the insight of a wise person. I did not say seek the insight of a family member or a friend. Seek the counsel of a wise person. If that wise person happens to be a friend or loved one, so be it. But being a friend or loved one does not automatically anoint someone as wise.

Be strong, my brothers and sisters. By brothers and sisters, I mean my brothers and sisters with whom I share this Earth. When we say brothers and sisters,

CONCLUSION

we make no distinction among black, white, yellow, brown, Christian, Buddhist, Hindu, Muslim, Jewish, atheist, or otherwise. The path in front of us may not be easy, but those who do not quit will be winners.

And now I would like to address the adults reading this book. We have to be vigilant about protecting ourselves and our youth. The *our* I am referring to here is a collective and communal *our*.

Fellow Americans, fellow adults, and fellow citizens, you are needed. To those who recognize, as I do, that discrimination is a heavy historical burden that we all carry in this country, I ask for your help. I am not asking you to state your opinion. I am asking you to search your heart and react. The data does not lie. Compared to their white peers, young black and brown males are being killed and abused by the police at alarming rates. The *why*—although critically important—has not been the subject of this book. It is the *what* that I am making this request about: What can each of us do to help?

To my conservative brothers and sisters, and less racially concerned brothers and sisters, I ask for your help, too. Let's for the sake of argument assume that whatever views you have about race are correct. What do we do? We still have a problem. Our fellow citizens, our comrades in the human experience, are being killed in unacceptably high numbers. The facts don't lie. We have a segment of the population that is being devastated physically and emotionally. As I've said, many conservatives want to argue, "What about black-on- black crime? Let's do something about that first." I would suggest that we need to work in parallel; that wherever people are being killed, there is a grave problem needing to be fixed. At this moment in time, we must assist in saving the lives of our young black, brown, and white brothers. From my perspective, if it were not black and brown males being abused, it would be another group of people. Let's work together to fix this before it spills over to other areas.

We are the United States of America. United we rise, and united we fall. In a nation as great and as interwoven in cultural diversity as ours, we will all rise together—or we will all fall together. There is no leaving one group behind and still expecting our nation to be as strong as it can be. There is acumen to the old adage: We, you, your family, your organization are only as strong as your weakest link. To put it another way: All boats float in a rising tide, and all boats sink in receding water. Meaning, when you are as linked as we are in the United States, what affects one affects all. We have to expand our view of community to include the collective *us*. We have to mature and move beyond the white community/black community stale argument. We all have to view ourselves as one big community of the United States of America. And then, within that community, we have to recognize and celebrate our differences. We have to acknowledge that each of us needs something different and each of us has a vital role to play within the larger community.

Even the most hardened and mean soul can simultaneously not like blacks, but at the same time, love Michael Jordan. They find a way to make an exception for their learned predispositions. We all do it in all aspects of our lives. We just don't know we are doing it. So go out and find your Michael Jordan and help him. In the interest of the public good and in the spirit of doing what is right, reach out to any underserved community to someone who does not look like you. It is important to reach out to them with the perspective that we have something to mutually learn from one another. We are both going to benefit.

The good, the bad, and the indifferent in other people and in the world do not change our individual responsibility to be the best person we can be. No one's life is perfect. No hand that was dealt you absolves you of your responsibility to be the best person you can be and to do the right thing. As a black male growing up in America, I am uniquely aware, and can say without fear of contradiction, that life is not fair. However, I am also aware that life is not fair for anyone. And I was not put here to be the evaluator of whose unfairness is the gravest. I was put here to be the best me, regardless of circumstances.

Several years ago, while working a shift in the emergency department in a rural hospital, I treated an interesting patient. Let's name the patient Peter. Peter was a 65-year-old southern-appearing white male who presented to the nurse at the ER, complaining of chest pain that he had been feeling for 12 hours. Peter went on to explain, "I am farmer, and that is what I have done all my life. I live on my daddy's farm, and farming is how I make a living. I started to have chest pain this morning, and I felt kind of funny. My chest was hurting all day, but I did not want to come in until I tended to my farm." Peter said it took him 12 hours to do his farm work and his chest was hurting the entire time.

The nurse let me know I had a patient with chest pain waiting to be evaluated. When I saw him, Peter was not rude to me, but he was very distant. I conducted a full history and performed a full physical exam. The nurse did the electrocardiogram (EKG) and brought it to me right away. The EKG showed that Peter was having an acute myocardial infarction, also known as a heart attack. In medicine, we sometimes call Peter's particular set of symptoms a "widow maker," meaning that according to the EKG, he most likely had two to three coronary vessels clogged. Peter needed immediate care and needed to be transferred to the closest cardiac center.

I informed Peter that he was having the worst kind of heart attack and I needed to give him lifesaving medicine and transfer him to a cardiac center. To my utter amazement, Peter calmly got up and started getting dressed and muttered he would be just fine. I began to attempt to convince him to stay and shared that he would likely die if he left. Peter was still oddly distant and acted as if he did not really hear me. There was something strange, but familiar, about his behavior. Peter was putting on his shoes, and I informed him that I needed him to sign an "against medical advice" (AMA) form. I explained to him the form basically states that the physician has professionally recommended a course of treatment consistent with acceptable standards of care and has recommended immediate admission to a cardiac center. It also said that I had explained the risk of leaving against medical advice. Peter agreed to wait and let me retrieve the form.

I left the room and found Tom. Tom was a 30ish-year-old white male tech who had never gone to college. His main role in the emergency department was to assist the nurses, physicians, and the entire emergency department team. I knew Tom well and had taken care of his children a few times. I asked Tom to do me a favor. I had Tom put on a long white coat that did not have a name or title on it. I explained to Tom that I simply needed him to go into Peter's room and, in

Peter's presence, thumb through his chart, look at the EKG, and then say to Peter, "Sir, you are having a large heart attack. It is imperative that we treat you and then transfer you." I instructed Tom not to say anything more, not to answer any questions, and to immediately leave the room after saying this. Tom did just what I requested of him.

A few minutes after Tom left the room, I returned with the AMA papers, and Peter was lying on the gurney with the hospital gown on. He said to me, "I will stay and be treated." Tom was given a thrombolytic (clot dissolving medicine) and transferred to a local heart center, where he received a cardiac catheterization that opened his clogged arteries. The cardiologist called to thank me for the referral, which is typical. But the cardiologist went on to say that Peter's vessels were completely occluded and he would have undoubtedly died without prompt treatment.

What I sensed during my initial evaluation of Peter was something indescribably familiar. I had assessed that if a white male, rather than a black male, told Peter that he needed to stay to be treated, he would likely stay. I understood that it could have been all in my mind, but my intuition told me to try the experiment anyway.

I had no clinical obligation to do what I did. In fact, a medical ethicist could argue what I did was wrong. But I had to do what I could to save Peter's life, which for me was clearly the right things to do. I am a part of the human family, and so is Peter. Being a family member at that moment meant not allowing what I could have taken as a personal offense to distract me from my obligation to my fellow human and to the extended family of humans. My, your, and all of our obligations are simple: Do the right thing. Extend yourself beyond what you're technically obligated to do or not do, and do what is right in the best interest of America and humanity. Seek to be a miracle for someone else.

We will *all* need help in ways that we cannot predict. We are also called to help people in ways that the people we're helping can't predict, and may never even know about, just as Peter never knew how I had helped him. We don't do this for the sake of recognition. No, we do this because we are humans. When we help one person, we create a spirit or energy that goes on and helps many more.

We may not experience the benefit of our positive actions or selfless giving, but someone else will benefit. It is important that we pay it forward. And, one day, we or our loved ones will benefit from a good that someone else has put into the world.

Let's all strive to make this a better place to live. Let's make ourselves better. And when we become better selves, we become a better country. It does not matter what color, race, or religion we are. We are all on a journey together. The journey is to make this a better country and a better world.

Let's all make America greater. A journey of a thousand miles begins with a single step. Let's take that step together.

REFERENCES

Allen, James. *As a Man Thinketh.* New York: Chartwell Books, 2015.

Breul, Nick, and Keith, Mike, "Deadly Calls and Fatal Encounters." National Law Enforcement Officers Memorial Fund, 2016. http://www.nleomf.org/assets/pdfs/officer-safety/Primary_Research_Final_11-0_updated_8_31_16.pdf

Coates, Ta-Nehisi, *Between the World and Me.* New York: Spiegel & Grau, 2015.

Dunbar, Paul Laurence, "We Wear the Mask." Poetry Foundation. https://www.poetryfoundation.org/poems/44203/we-wear-the-mask (accessed May 21, 2018)

Dyson, Michael Eric, *The Black Presidency: Barack Obama and the Politics of Race in America.* New York: Houghton Mifflin Harcourt, 2017.

Ellison, Ralph, *Invisible Man.* New York: Random House, 1952.

Epp, Charles R.; Maynard-Moody, Steven; and Haider-Markel, Donald P. *Pulled Over: How Police Stops Define Race and Citizenship.* Chicago: The University of Chicago Press, 2014.

Ferner, Matt, and Wing, Nick, "Here's How Many Cops Got Convicted of Shootings Last Year." *The Huffington Post*, January 13, 2016. https://www.huffingtonpost.com/entry/police-shooting-convictions_us_5695968ce4b086bc1cd5d0da

Gladwell, Malcolm, *Outliers: The Story of Success.* New York: Little, Brown and Company, 2008.

Greenlea, Sam. *The Spook Who Sat by the Door*. New York: Brawtley Press, 2015.

Guest, Edgar, "Don't Quit." All Creatures. http://www.all-creatures.org/poetry/dontquit.html (accesed May 21, 2018)

Hauler, Leslie. "5 Facts About Police Brutality in the United States That Will Shock You." AOL, October 22, 2015. https://www.aol.com/article/2015/10/22/5-facts-about-police-brutality-in-the-united-states-that-will-sh/21252144/

Henley, William Ernest, "Invictus." Poetry Foundation. https://www.poetryfoundation.org/poems/51642/invictus (accessed May 21, 2018)

Jay-Z, "99 Problems." *The Black Album*. New York: Def Jam Records, 2004.

Kipling, Rudyard, "If—" *Poetry Foundation.* https://www.poetryfoundation.org/poems/46473/if--- (accessed May 21, 2018).

Krieger, Nancy, et al. "Police Killings and Police Deaths Are Public Health Data and Can Be Counted." Public Library of Science, December 8, 2015. http://journals.plos.org/plosmedicine/article?id=10.1371/journal.pmed.1001915

Lartey, Jamiles. (2015, July 9). "By the Numbers: US Police Kill More in Days than Other Countries Do in Years." *The Guardian,* June 9, 2015. https://www.theguardian.com/us-news/2015/jun/09/the-counted-police-killings-us-vs-other-countries

"Law Enforcement Facts." National Law Enforcement Officers Fund. http://www.nleomf.org/facts/enforcement/ (accessed May 21, 2018)

REFERENCES

Lee, Michelle Ye Hee, "Are Black or White Offenders More Likely to Kill Police? *The Washington Post,* January 9, 2015. https://www.washingtonpost.com/news/fact-checker/wp/2015/01/09/are-black-or-white-offenders-more-likely-to-kill-police/?noredirect=on&utm_term=.2db417cfa2f1

Mapping Police Violence. https://mappingpoliceviolence.org/ (accessed May 21, 2018).

"*Miranda* warning." Wikipedia. https://en.wikipedia.org/wiki/Miranda_warning (accessed May 21, 2018)

Mullainathan, Sendhil. Retrieved from "Police Killings of Blacks: Here Is What the Data Says." *The New York Times,* October 18, 2015. https://www.nytimes.com/2015/10/18/upshot/police-killings-of-blacks-what-the-data-says.html

Noble, Andrea, "Shooting Deaths of Police Up 78 Percent This Year." *The Washington Times, July 27, 2016.* https://www.washingtontimes.com/news/2016/jul/27/shooting-deaths-of-police-up-78-percent-this-year/

Public Enemy, "Don't Believe the Hype." *It Takes a Nation of Millions to Hold Us Back. New York: Def Jam Records, 1988.*

Simons, Janet, et al, "Maslow's Hierarchy of Human Needs," in *Psychology: The Search for Understanding. New York: West Publishing Company, 1987.*

Sloan, Frank, et al, "The Longevity Gap Between Black and White Men in the United States at the Beginning and End of the 20th Century." *American Journal of Public Health,* February 2010, pp. 357–363.

Swaine, Jon, et al, (2015, December 31). "Young Black Men Killed by US Police at Highest Rate in Year of 1,134

Deaths." *The Guardian,* December 31, 2015. https://www.theguardian.com/us-news/2015/dec/31/the-counted-police-killings-2015-young-black-men

"The Counted: People Killed by Police in the US." *The Guardian.* https://www.theguardian.com/us-news/ng-interactive/2015/jun/01/the-counted-police-killings-us-database (accessed May 21, 2018)

Tutu, Desmond, *The Book of Forgiving: The Fourfold Path for Healing Ourselves and Our World.* New York: HarperCollins, 2014.

Wong, Kathleen, "10 Police Brutality Statistics that are Absolutely Shocking." *Mic,* December 9, 2015. https://mic.com/articles/129981/10-police-brutality-statistics-that-are-absolutely-shocking#.pGtwtyH4E

Zukav, Gary, *The Seat of the Soul.* New York: Simon & Schuster, 1990.

Made in the USA
Monee, IL
20 March 2021